AMERICAN
WAR LIBRARY

★ ★ ★ ★

★ World War II ★

WEAPONS OF WAR

Lucent Books, P.O. Box 289011, San Diego, CA 92198-9011

Titles in The American War Library series include:

World War II
Hitler and the Nazis
Kamikazes
Leaders and Generals
Life as a POW
Life of an American Soldier in
  Europe
Strategic Battles in Europe
Strategic Battles in the Pacific
The War at Home
Weapons of War

The Civil War
Leaders of the North and South
Life Among the Soldiers and
  Cavalry
Lincoln and the Abolition of
  Slavery
Strategic Battles
Weapons of War

Library of Congress Cataloging-in-Publication Data

Weapons of war
     p.   cm.—(American war library. World War II)
Includes bibliographical references and index.
Summary: Discusses the weapons, tank combat, U-boat
activities, fighter planes, and campaigns of World War II.
ISBN 1-56006-584-2 (lib. bdg. : alk. paper)
1. World War, 1939–1945—Juvenile literature. 2. Weapons—
Juvenile literature. [1. World War, 1939–1945.] I. Title. II.
Series.
D743.7.N57   2000
940.53—dc21

99-053209

Copyright 2000 by Lucent Books, Inc.
P.O. Box 289011, San Diego, California 92198-9011

Printed in the U.S.A.

★ Contents ★

A Nation Forged by War

The United States, like many nations, was forged and defined by war. Despite Benjamin Franklin's opinion that "There never was a good war or a bad peace," the United States owes its very existence to the War of Independence, one to which Franklin wholeheartedly subscribed. The country forged by war in 1776 was tempered and made stronger by the Civil War in the 1860s.

The Texas Revolution, the Mexican-American War, and the Spanish-American War expanded the country's borders and gave it overseas possessions. These wars made the United States a world power, but this status came with a price, as the nation became a key but reluctant player in both World War I and World War II.

Each successive war further defined the country's role on the world stage. Following World War II, U.S. foreign policy redefined itself to focus on the role of defender, not only of the freedom of its own citizens, but also of the freedom of people everywhere. During the cold war that followed World War II until the collapse of the Soviet Union, defending the world meant fighting communism. This goal, manifested in the Korean and Vietnam conflicts, proved elusive, and soured the American public on its achievability. As the United States emerged as the world's sole superpower, American foreign policy has been guided less by national interest and more on protecting international human rights. But as involvement in Somalia and Kosovo prove, this goal has been equally elusive.

As a result, the country's view of itself changed. Bolstered by victories in World Wars I and II, Americans first relished the role of protector. But, as war followed war in a seemingly endless procession, Americans began to doubt their leaders, their motives, and themselves. The Vietnam War especially caused people to question the validity of sending its young people to die in places where they were not particularly wanted and for people who did not seem especially grateful.

While the most obvious changes brought about by America's wars have been geopolitical in nature, many other aspects of society have been touched. War often does not bring about change directly, but acts instead like the catalyst in a chemical reaction, accelerating changes already in progress.

Some of these changes have been societal. The role of women in the United States had been slowly changing, but World War II put thousands into the workforce and into uniform. They might have gone back to being housewives after the war, but equality, once experienced, would not be forgotten.

Likewise, wars have accelerated technological change. The necessity for faster airplanes and a more destructive bomb led to the development of jet planes and nuclear energy. Artificial fibers developed for parachutes in the 1940s were used in the clothing of the 1950s.

Lucent Books' American War Library covers key wars in the development of the nation. Each war is covered in several volumes, to allow for more detail, context, and to provide volumes on often neglected subjects, such as the kamikazes of World War II, or weapons used in the Civil War. As with all Lucent Books, notes, annotated bibliographies, and appendixes such as glossaries give students a launching point for further research. In addition, sidebars and archival photographs enhance the text. Together, each volume in The American War Library will aid students in understanding how America's wars have shaped and changed its politics, economics, and society.

Improving Modern Warfare

Armies of the First World War pioneered many new technologies that would forever change the way battles would be fought: the airplane, the tank, the submarine, and even the aircraft carrier. Although these weapons quickly became indispensable on the modern battlefield, their futures were initially uncertain. During World War I the senior members of the military tended to cling to the proven weapons of the past such as mounted cavalry, distrusting the effectiveness of modern innovations that were still in their infancy. It wasn't until the Second World War that the true potential of these new weapons was fully realized. Tanks, which had lumbered across trench lines supporting infantry in World War I, became highly mobile and independent forces that spearheaded through enemy territory, often leaving friendly infantry struggling to keep up. And at sea, the aircraft carrier, a once ungainly and dangerous experiment, revolutionized naval warfare when admiralties realized that airpower

could negate the strategy of building bigger, more heavily armored battleships to rule the oceans.

Such technological advances irreversibly changed the way war was conducted. The static battlefields of the First World War gave way to the mechanized arenas of WWII where, owing to the concert of airpower, armored units, and ground troops, terrain was won and lost on a regular basis. Naval conflicts that once required opposing sides to line up to pummel each other were superseded by engagements in which, thanks to the striking distance of naval aircraft, the surface fleets rarely saw each other. The one aspect that didn't change, however, was the manpower that decided how these weapons were employed in battle. After all, most of these weapons in their more modern form were completely untested in warfare. It was the skill of the pilot, the tank officer, and the common infantryman with his rifle that demonstrated how effective a weapon could be. And it was men, not machines, who would ultimately have to seize the enemy's ground in order to claim victory.

To tout the contributions of the common soldier, however, is unnecessary. The bravery and skill of men in battle are unquestioned. But even these soldiers benefited from the weapons they possessed. The common American GI carried an M1 Garand rifle, a semiautomatic weapon capable of firing eight cartridges before needing to be reloaded. The rapid rate of fire was clearly superior to the single-shot, bolt-action rifles used by all other armies in the war. Thus technology gave the Americans an added edge in a firefight. And despite those who may contend that weapons accomplish their aim no matter how primitive or modern or how large or small, improvements in weapons certainly helped decide the fortunes of war. As author Chris Bishop comments,

> In short, many would simply say that guns are guns, bombs are bombs, aircraft are aircraft, and so on. But there is certainly more to it than that, for the capacity to win or lose a war actually rested on these weapons' qualities, just as much as it did on the fighting skills of those who employed them and on the strategic sense of those who directed them in their use.[1]

Although a few weapons of World War II foreshadowed the turning tide in warfare, many remained part of the conventional concept of combat. The German V-1 and V-2 rockets that fell on England prefigured the guided missiles of today's battlefield, and the atomic bombs dropped on Hiroshima and Nagasaki to force Japan's surrender proved to be an ominous ancestor to the nuclear weapons that still threaten the world at large. These weapons removed the personal aspect

A U.S. Navy dive-bomber attacks a Japanese cruiser in the Pacific. In World War II, surface fleets rarely saw each other during battle.

Carrying his M1 Garand rifle, a U.S. marine advances on an enemy position. The Garand's rapid rate of fire gave Americans an advantage in combat.

from warfare; they required no skill to accomplish their deadly tasks. Yet the tanks and planes that engaged the enemy were manned by human beings. To compete with the enemy forces and stay alive, the militaries of all the warring nations strove to make these conventional weapons better and better. And because of the ingenuity of design that was apparent in the battlefield, these weapons—the tanks, the aircraft, the ships—will long be remembered as characterizing the Second World War.

✶ Chapter 1 ✶

The Tank: Armored Blitzkrieg

O ne of the most memorable words to come out of World War II was *blitzkrieg*. A German term for "lightning war," the blitzkrieg was a new method of attack that had both strategic and tactical dimensions. On the larger, strategic level, the blitzkrieg called for a rapid strike by combined air and ground forces in an attempt to overwhelm the enemy and drive deep into their lines, causing them great confusion and forcing them to continually fall back to counter the penetration. "The way to achieve this lay not in bigger, less mobile and, of necessity, fewer weapons," historian Ward Rutherford explains, "but in large numbers of small, faster-moving ones always used in close combination."[2] On the battlefield, or tactical level, lightning war relied on four elements: airpower to destroy strong points; artillery to soften up defenses and demoralize the enemy soldiers; infantry to effect a breech in the defender's lines; and, finally, armored units to drive through the breech and encircle the enemy lines, seize strategic positions (such as road junctures, rail lines, etc.), and continue deeper into enemy territory.

The German army used the blitzkrieg in many theaters of war. The term became inseparable from the successful 1939 assault on Poland, which, because of the combined operations, forced that country to surrender after only two weeks of fighting. It also characterized the attack on France and the Low Countries in 1940, which brought one of Germany's historical rivals to its knees in roughly a month. And though ultimately a failure in the Russian campaign, the blitzkrieg tactics garnered Germany's initial successes in the invasion of that nation in 1941. The two military innovations that made the blitzkrieg such a dreaded but effective type of combat were precision tactical bombers and fast, powerful armored tanks.

The New Armored Warfare

In World War I airplanes had limited and ineffective bombing capabilities; by the Sec-

A German armored unit advances into France during the blitzkrieg. The use of tanks helped defeat France in about four weeks.

ond World War, the tactical bomber had come of age, and the German air force, the Luftwaffe, used the new tool to its advantage. But airplanes could not hold enemy territory. They could disrupt, demoralize, and destroy, but they could not force an enemy into retreat or occupy the vacated land. The German armored units, or panzer divisions, could accomplish both of these tasks and more. Born out of the lumbering World War I tanks that were designed to break the stalemate of trench warfare in the late 1910s, the more advanced tank units that swept across Poland and France had a similar purpose—to restore mobility to the battlefield.

Unlike their predecessors, the tanks of World War II were relatively fast. The typical behemoth of the First World War plodded along at 10 miles per hour (mph); the mainstay of the German panzer division in 1940—the Panzerkampfwagen (Pzkw) Mark III—cruised at 40 mph. Another important distinction was that most of the new tanks had turrets to give their armament a 360-degree traverse. Speed and the rotating gun

Unlike the tanks of the First World War (left), German panzers (below) were fast, maneuverable, and had their guns mounted in movable turrets.

gave panzers the ability to fire in any direction while on the move. This provided the tank with an offensive capability while it defensively maneuvered to avoid enemy fire. It was an effective combination that made the tank a powerful weapon on the battlefield.

Germany was certainly not the only country to be developing tanks and tank warfare at the outset of World War II. Britain had spearheaded tank design and manufacture in the First World War, but, by September 1939, it had few tanks in service that could outperform their German counterparts. Britain's vast number of light tanks carried weapons that could not penetrate the 30-millimeter (mm) armor of the best German tanks. The British A-13 mounted a 2-pounder turret gun that could contend with the German tanks, but it had weak armor, leaving it easy prey to the German Pzkw III's 37-mm and the Pzkw IV's 75-mm guns. The British did possess the Matilda infantry support tank, which carried thick armor and an effective 2-pounder, but by war's beginning, Britain had only twenty-three of these models in service. France also had armored divisions in its arsenal, but the French tank design—much like its entire military strategy—accentuated defense. Its huge Char B was nearly as well plated as the Matilda and it mounted two powerful guns (one in the turret and the other in the fore deck of the vehicle), but the immense weight of the tank allowed for little mobility. German tank crews learned not to face thesc giants in their Pzkw IIIs or IVs but instead waited for Stuka dive-bombers to eliminate the crawling beasts from the air.

The Successful Panzers

In an effort to design the best tanks, all nations throughout the war battled with the same problems: how to maximize firepower and armor thickness while still keeping the vehicle moving at a respectable speed. From 1939 through 1940, each combatant had its set of light tanks that could travel fast but could not stand up to a fight because either they lacked a powerful enough gun or their armor was so thin that they could be easily destroyed. The French and British also possessed heavy tanks that could slug it out in battle, but they were easily outmaneuvered or fell victim to air attacks because they were so slow. All sides did have main battle tanks that seemed to have good tradeoffs between armor, weapon, and speed, leaving them to

A Panzerkampfwagen Mark IV displays its formidable 75-mm gun. The British and French had few tanks that could match the Pzkw IV.

face the enemy tanks on equal terms. However, in nearly all of the armored engagements in the opening years of the war, the Germans were victorious even when the tanks of both sides were well matched. Thus the explanation for the infamous success of Germany's panzer units had to lie outside of the tanks themselves.

The effectiveness of Germany's panzers was the result of many factors, all of which affected armored combat in the earlier stages of the war. First, the employment of tanks on the battlefield had to evolve. In World War I, tanks were conceived of as infantry support vehicles meant to break static warfare; they were not thought of as forces that could operate independent of the infantry. General Heinz Guderian, the brilliant German general who revised the role of tanks in World War II, ignored the restraints placed on tanks and organized independent armored divisions that could function without the support of the less mobile infantry columns. These divisions could exploit the holes punched in enemy lines and then filter through en masse to disrupt communications, threaten enemy artillery stationed behind the lines, or turn on the enemy from behind.

Second, the tank's aggressive power lay in its ability to maneuver, so Guderian's tactics required open spaces to be successful—an advantage they had in the fields of Poland and France, in the open deserts of North Africa, and on the vast Russian steppes. In confined spaces, such as in cities or woods, the tank was vulnerable because

undetected infantry could get close enough to the vehicle to employ antitank devices like grenades, bazookas, or mines.

The third factor that contributed to Germany's early success was the Allied armies' outdated tactics. As military artist John Batchelor asserts, "In numbers the Allies were superior to the Germans; in quality of equipment they were, on balance, about equal; in strategic and tactical application, they were markedly inferior."[3] Although the British and French had tanks of equal or superior make, their tanks clung to the role of

Panzers invade Poland. To successfully exploit the power of their tanks, armored divisions needed open spaces to maneuver.

infantry support. They had not created large tank divisions with multiple vehicles working in concert to overcome the enemy. Instead, they often fielded fewer tanks and relegated them to supporting the infantry, which bore the brunt of an attack. They also had not yet developed the blitzkrieg doctrine of combined arms, accomplishing armored breakthrough with the aid of tactical air support, artillery barrages, and infantry assault. In the opening stages of World War II, the foresight of German leaders and the well-disciplined tactics of the German military, combined with favorable terrain on which to fight, helped make Poland and France fall in short order, and provided many victories in North Africa and Russia.

The Russians: Masters of Improvisation

With France conquered and Britain on the run in North Africa, Adolf Hitler turned the full weight of his military on Russia in 1941. German panzer divisions, imbued with the spirit of recent victories, plunged across the open Russian steppes in unstoppable waves. The older Pzkw IIIs with 37-mm guns were being replaced with newer models carrying 50-mm cannon. The tactics were the same, and the victories in Russia came just as easily in 1941 as they had in France in 1940. The Russians had nearly six times the number of tanks that the Germans possessed, yet the tide fell in the Germans' favor for all the aforementioned reasons. In addition, the Russians were at a decided disadvantage in two other respects: Their early tanks had no

wireless communications, which made it difficult to work in concert or to receive orders from command units, and their officers in the command units were mostly unseasoned men, because Russian leader Joseph Stalin had purged the officer corps of many of its top men in an effort to eliminate potential dissidents. As a result, the Russian tank corps was a disorganized mass. But the Russians had embraced armored warfare in much the way Germany had.

The Russian armored command had its share of ineffectual light tanks and "land battleships" that were too slow to utilize their great strength, but it was constantly toying with new prototypes to make the best of speed, armor, and firepower. It found an effective combination in two designs. The first of these was the KV-I, which fielded a 76-mm gun in a well-armored turret. The armament was more powerful than anything the Germans possessed, and the front armor was thick enough to withstand shells from all but the dreaded 88-mm German antiaircraft gun that was pressed successfully into an antitank role. The KV-I had been around since 1940. Its more famous partner, the T-34/76, arrived on the battlefield in 1941. This second main counter to the German panzer carried the same gun as the KV-I (denoted by the "/76"), but it had less armor in order to give the tank greater mobility. Its armored hull, however, was sloped, deflecting all but the most carefully aimed shots from the 50-mm and 75-mm cannon of the Pzkw IIIs and IVs. (The sloped contour would continue to influence armor design throughout

Eighteen to One

In a small village near Moscow in the winter of 1941, Lieutenant Pavel Gudz and his crew gained fame in the Russian tank corps for engaging eighteen enemy tanks in their lone KV-IA. The Russian tank's thick armor and 76-mm gun, coupled with Gudz's discipline and skill, proved that the Soviets would not be as easy to overrun as the Germans had predicted. British historian George Forty relates the tale of Gudz and his KV-I in the book *Tank Action*.

Lt Gudz arranged for the artillery to put down a noisy barrage, underneath which he managed to move his tank, unheard and unseen, into a suitable ambush position. Now the enemy began moving out of the village and Lt Gudz decided to take on the lead tank, reasoning that "a burning tank at the head of their column would be visible to all of those following it". He gave the command: "On the leader, armour piercing [shell], aim for the joint, FIRE!" The tank shuddered and rocked on its suspension, while commander and gunner watched anxiously through their sights. The gunner, Lt Starykh, made a few minor corrections then fired again and they saw the lead tank lit up by a brilliant flash, then, less than 15 seconds later, it burst into flames. Starykh immediately engaged the next one in line. The second tank also began to smoke without having fired a shot. . . .

However, this finally gave away their ambush position and shortly afterwards the tank ". . . rang with a terrible noise and Gudz felt as though someone had hit his tanker's helmet with a sledge hammer, after which the lights went out". A shell had struck the glacis plate and bounced off. "Blessed were the hands of those steelworkers who had made this shell-proof steel!"

Lt Gudz and his crew kept on firing at the enemy until, after firing some three dozen rounds, the smoke and fumes inside the tank became almost unbearable. . . . They were now continually hit by enemy fire, but not one round penetrated. Five enemy tanks were on fire in the village, illuminating it from end to end. Three more tried to leave the village, but as they left the cover of the houses, Lt Gudz and his crew knocked them out.. "Eight cheery bonfires, eight glowing torches!". . .

He blasted another two at the edge of the village, while the remaining eight frantically tried to escape. By now the KV was almost out of ammunition and had been hit on its side armour, blowing off one of its road wheels. Gudz ordered the tank to be pulled back, slowly, so as not to lose a track and

when it returned to its starting position it did not appear to be the same machine. It was missing fenders, fuel tanks, tool bins and spare track links. . . . Two days later Pavel Gudz and his battalion commander showed the front newspaper correspondent the tank, where he could personally count twenty-nine hits on its armour.

For his part in the battle on 5 December 1941 in the village of Nefedevo, Lt Pavel Danilovich Gudz was awarded the Order of Lenin.

the modern period.) Heinz Guderian was one of many experts who marveled at the simple design. The T-34 could be mass-produced easily and cheaply. An entire arsenal in the Russian city of Kirov was devoted to churning out nothing but that tank. A German armor officer, Colonel Hans von Luck, conceded,

The T-34 was an uncomplicated construction. Its armor plates were welded crudely together, its transmission was simple, everything without any great frills or finesse. Damage was easy to repair. In addition, the Russians were masters of improvisation. Thousands upon thousands of the T-34s were produced, in factories that lay beyond the reach of our Luftwaffe.[4]

The Gun/Armor Spiral

The T-34/76 proved to be the equal of the early model German Pzkw IV on the battlefield, so both Germany and Russia came out with variants of their main tanks in an attempt to keep one step ahead of their opponents in terms of firepower and armor thickness. This was the classic struggle that pervaded nearly every nation that manufactured tanks, but it was perhaps most obvious in the Russian campaign. Historians refer to the impetus behind the race to come out with better tanks as the gun/armor spiral. Essentially the gun/armor spiral was a competition. When the German Pzkw IV's short-barrel 75-mm gun proved less than effective against the armor of the T-34, its gun was replaced by a high-powered 75-mm long-barreled cannon. In addition, the new Pzkw IV was given thicker armor to withstand shots from the T-34's 76-mm gun. In response to this new threat, the T-34/76 un-

derwent its own modifications to maintain equality. The third variant, or T-34/76c, with 60-mm armor and an improved 76-mm gun, kept the competition alive.

Although the Germans continued to make improvements to the Pzkw IV (it was, as Denis Bishop and Christopher Ellis note, "destined to be the only tank of any nation to remain in production throughout World War II"[5]), their engineers' next move was to try an entirely new design. The fruit of their labor was the Pzkw V Panther. The Panther was perhaps the best medium tank of the war. It copied the T-34's sloped-armor hull but possessed a frontal armor thickness of 120 millimeters. It also boasted a high-velocity long-barreled 75-mm gun that could penetrate nearly every tank created

These Soviet T-34 tanks are about to be transported to the front. The T-34 had sloped armor that deflected all but the most carefully aimed enemy shells.

during the war years. Since the T-34/76's rather stubby gun could not hope to open up a Panther's armor, the Soviets upgraded their tank with an 85-mm cannon and christened it the T-34/85. The T-34/85 was capable of knocking out the Panther, but it was not assured. The hunt for bigger and better tanks continued on both sides.

Britain Tries to Catch Up

The British had been left out of the early stages of competition primarily because their existing tanks were not capable of being upgraded. As Major Kenneth J. Mack-sey writes, "The British had found themselves to have been less well served when it was discovered that their prewar tanks were hard pressed to accept heavier guns and armour. The Matilda was quite incapable of being up-gunned and had to go out of production when the gun/armour race got too hot."[6] Unlike the Germans and the Russians, who had to make only slight modifications to the existing Pzkw IV and T-34 chassis, the British had to start from scratch to come up with tanks that could hold their own against the Germans.

Shot and Shell

One aspect of the gun/armor spiral was the need to constantly improve the types of shell used to penetrate enemy armor. In the following passage, the authors of *Tanks and Weapons of World War II* describe the various ways in which antitank munitions were altered to increase their chances of punching through the thick armor plating of an opponent's tank.

Into the design of shot and shell went enormous research. Simple armour-piercing shot (and even larger calibre high-explosive shells) was able to penetrate or disrupt light armour, but thicker armour with specially hardened faces could only be defeated by sophisticated shot moving at very high velocities. For instance, early British shot was found to break up against German face-hardened armour, a process that could be prevented if the shot were made stronger, fitted with a protective cap, or given a higher velocity—usually a combination of all three. Rises in velocity were the most common solution . . . , brought about either by increasing the size of charge relative to projectile . . . or squeezing the round [through a tapered gun barrel].

But a quite different approach to armour penetration from that practised by the brute force of high-velocity, kinetic-energy rounds came with chemical-energy ammunitions—the hollow charge or high-explosive anti-tank (HEAT) rounds. These low-velocity projectiles . . . exploded on the hostile armour and then directed a jet of molten debris to cut a thin hole at something like 27,000 feet per second. Not only could they be fired from ordinary [tank] guns, but also from the hand-held infantry weapons such as [American] Bazooka, [British] Piat, and [German] Panzerfaust; and though they had a somewhat lower chance of killing a tank than shot, they could cut through the thickest armour, and, being cheap and easy to make, proliferated the number of anti-tank weapons infesting the battlefield.

In the interim, the British did the next best thing. They bought tanks from the United States and converted them to compete with the Germans. In 1941, the British were fighting German ground forces only in North Africa but were losing that war—in part because their tanks were proving inferior. A modified American M3 Stuart light tank was the first to reach the deserts and help stem the Germans and their Italian allies. The British dubbed their version the Honey, and it carried a high-velocity 37-mm gun—though somewhat outdated, the long, tapered bore improved the shell's penetration. The Honeys were faster than most of their German counterparts, which helped to keep them alive and gave them the mobility to outflank the enemy tanks. They were too light, however, to bring the German panzers to a standstill.

That job was accomplished gradually by two tanks. The first, the British M3 General Grant, a modified American M3 General Lee with a 37-mm gun in the turret and a strong 75-mm gun in the right side of the front hull, appeared in 1942. The Grant had 57-mm armor, making it all but impervious to the German 37-mm and 50-mm guns of the Pzkw IIIs still in use. The second—and more important—tank was the M4 General Sherman. The Sherman maintained its name under British use and was first used to great effect in the Battle of El Alamein, where the British finally halted the German

An American M4 General Sherman tank races across the desert of North Africa. The Sherman's chief advantage was that it was easy to build and repair.

advance eastward across North Africa. The Sherman had the basic hull structure of a Lee but it carried only a turret-mounted 75-mm gun. The Sherman was easier to build than the Lee and its 75-mm gun had full traverse, whereas the Lee's heavy gun had a limited arc while stuck in its forward hull. The Sherman was fairly impervious to the lighter guns of many German tanks, but it was not unstoppable. The 88-mm antiaircraft gun, which had proved itself capable of destroying even the heaviest Russian, French, and British tanks, could blow a Sherman up at a range of one thousand yards. The later variants of the Pzkw IV, with their long-barrel 75-mm guns, were also effective against the Sherman. But the true value of the Sherman came in its numbers.

The Shermans were easy to build and repair, and the United States could churn out thousands of them to sell to their new ally, Britain.

America Enters the War

America entered the Second World War in December 1941 when the Japanese bombed Pearl Harbor. Since Japan was allied with the Axis powers of Germany and Italy, America's arsenal was faced with fighting all three. The Pacific Theater, with its dense jungle fighting, was not conducive to tank combat. The Japanese did possess a few types of tanks, but their armor and armament were too light to contend with the American vehicles sent to the region. Most of the fighting in the islands of the Pacific was accomplished by the foot soldier, with tanks playing less of a role.

In 1943, however, American tank forces were engaged against Axis forces in North Africa. Landings in Morocco brought U.S. power to the aid of the British army still fighting in the deserts along the African coast. The Americans had mostly Shermans in their arsenal, but they were supplemented by a few M10 tank destroyers, open-topped vehicles with light armor but a fairly powerful 76-mm gun. Facing the German and Italian armies for the first time, the Americans were unprepared, and many Shermans were lost to the well-trained Axis forces.

Besides the deadly 88-mm antiaircraft gun, the Germans possessed new Tiger tanks

The M10 tank destroyer was based on the design of the M4 Sherman. It had an open turret equipped with a 76-mm gun.

that mounted 88-mm guns in their turrets. Perhaps the most feared and famous of the German heavy tanks, the Tiger weighed fifty-five tons and carried armor 110 millimeters thick on several parts of its hull. Yet the Tiger was rushed into service in 1942, and its kinks had not been worked out by the time it faced the Americans. Major Macksey explains that, although the Tiger "enjoyed material superiority over any armoured vehicle then in the war, the violent haste of development and production gave vent to a nagging unreliability which, all too often, left undamaged machines in Allied hands during the recurring withdrawals."[7] In addition, like all tanks, the awesome Tiger was vulnerable from the air. British and American planes that established mastery over the African skies began "tank busting," hunting the German armor before it could reach the battlefield.

The same feats were to be repeated when Allied armies invaded Italy in 1943 and France in 1944. The German tanks were getting progressively better armed and better armored, but the Allied air forces controlled the skies, leaving the Germans less room to maneuver without exposing themselves to attack from above. Essentially, Germany was on the defensive. It couldn't adopt blitzkrieg tactics anymore, so the German tanks evolved to fit a defensive role. Speed was no longer an issue; the tradeoff

British troops examine an abandoned German Tiger tank. The Tiger's unreliability was due to its hasty development and manufacture.

between more armor and less mobility was worthwhile for the Germans late in the war. For the Allies, the opposite was true. The British and American designers built tanks knowing that they would need to be fast enough to move through Italy and France. As Germany had done years before, the Allies recognized that only by plunging deep into enemy territory and seizing cities, railways, and industrial sites could they wreck the German war effort.

To this effect, the Americans maintained production of the fast, sturdy Sherman, though they upgraded its armor and gun through successive variants. The Sherman continued to prove itself in European battlefields—despite the fact that it was easy to destroy—because it was well built, easy to repair, and could still be mass-produced. As

U.S. general Omar Bradley attested, "It was in dependability that the American tank clearly outclassed the German; its powerful engine could always be counted on to run without a breakdown."[8] Some 49,234 Shermans either filled the ranks of American armored divisions or were sold to the British and Russian armies. In their typical desire to improve on the American designs, the British came out with an excellent variant of the Sherman called the Firefly, which boasted a 17-pound cannon that had penetration nearly equal to the German 88-mm gun. Other than the Sherman, the United States developed the M18 Hellcat to fill the role of a fast tank destroyer, the role previously occupied by the M10. The Hellcat was poorly armored but it weighed only 20 tons, giving it an incredible top speed of 55 mph. Like most U.S. vehicles, it was designed for "hit and run" attacks and not meant to stand up to the obviously superior German panzers in a firefight.

GIs ride a German Tiger II tank captured during the Battle of the Bulge. Its slow speed and high rate of fuel consumption offset the King Tiger's awesome power.

Germany on the Defensive

Germany was also concentrating on tank destroyers toward the end of the war for two reasons. First, the thin-skinned, open-topped, turretless models were perfect for defensive purposes where terrain or improved earthen ditches could be used to compensate for their light armor. Second, these vehicles, fitted to older chassis and requiring less armor and no turret hydraulics, were much easier to manufacture than the fully enclosed heavy tanks. Affixing an 88-mm gun to an open-topped Nashorn ("Rhinoceros") tank destroyer was much cheaper and easier than welding one inside the turret of a Tiger.

The proliferation of tank destroyers did not stop Germany from continuing to experiment with heavy tanks, however. The 68-ton Tiger II, or King Tiger, was one of the most powerful tanks of the war. It had front armor 185 millimeters thick. Few, if any, Allied tank guns could penetrate it. It also mounted its predecessor's impressive 88-mm gun, which could still destroy nearly every vehicle in the Allied arsenal. The Germans used these fearsome machines during the Battle of the Bulge, the last major German counterattack in the Western European Theater. Full of hope and audacity, the Germans tried to drive the Allied armies in the Ardennes Forest back to the sea. The plan met with initial success but ultimately failed, in part because the huge new heavy tanks were not swift enough to drive deep into enemy territory and their high fuel-consumption rate meant that they constantly ran out of gas. When the Allied planes took to the air in retribution, the lumbering giants were picked off one by one.

The Russian Juggernaut

Continuing their gun/armor competition with the Germans, the Russians began producing heavier and heavier tanks in 1943. The JS-II (Joseph Stalin II) was perhaps the best of the Russian tanks to come out of the late war years. It had armor up to 132 millimeters thick on its front hull, yet it weighed only 45 tons. It could stand up to nearly everything the Germans had on the eastern front. One panzer officer was frustrated when his powerful Tiger tanks had their first encounter with the heavily armored JS-IIs. "Although my Tigers began hitting them at 2,200 yards," he recalled, "our shells did not penetrate until half that distance."[9] The drawback to the JS-II was that it had only twenty-eight rounds of ammunition in its storage rack for its 122-mm gun. Since the individual vehicles could not participate in a long firefight without running out of shells, the Russians had to field quite a few tanks to be effective.

By 1944, the Russians had the industrial capacity to create vast numbers of tanks. The Germans were being pushed out of Soviet lands and back into Poland, allowing Russian factories to operate unabated. They produced thousands of heavy tanks, including the new JSU-122 tank destroyer and JSU-152 assault gun. Both were turretless but enclosed vehicles: The JSU-122 had an awesome 122-mm gun mounted in the hull, while the JSU-152 carried a 152-mm short-barreled howitzer designed for annihilating infantry but which quite capably punched through enemy tanks as well. Along with the turreted JS-II, these heavy, well-armored vehicles overwhelmed the Germans, who were fielding fewer and fewer tanks as the war dragged on.

Production Carries the Day

Toward the end of the war, the Germans were failing to keep pace with the Allied armor production. One reason was that British and American bombing raids on Germany's industrial heartland were damaging some tank factories and destroying other factories that manufactured the raw materials needed to build tanks. But German production was never seriously hampered for long periods of time, so other, more crippling factors were primarily to blame. The first significant factor was the Allied control of the skies. The new rocket-armed fighter planes and improved tactical

Wittman at Villers-Bocage

By the time German tank ace Michael Wittman reached the fighting in Normandy in 1944, he had already claimed 117 kills in France and Russia. Most of his victories were scored in his Pzkw VI Tiger, and it was this infamous vehicle that he brought to the Normandy region on June 12, six days after the Allies had landed on the French coast. In this excerpt from his book *Tank Action*, George Forty describes the melee that ensued when Wittman's small tank brigade encountered a British armored column that had temporarily halted along a road outside the quiet town of Villers-Bocage.

> Wittman, having seen the stationary tanks, decided to leave the rest of his force and cut around behind the enemy in his Tiger, in order to take a closer look at Villers-Bocage and size up the situation. Entering from the east, he immediately spotted the four Cromwells of RHQ 4CLY [tanks of the regimental headquarters of a unit of sharpshooters], parked in the main street, knocked out three of them . . . but the fourth managed to escape by getting off the road into the garden of a house. . . .

> [After destroying the remaining vehicles in the headquarters unit], Wittman turned round and moved back eastward. He then met the fourth RHQ tank which had been stalking him, hoping to get a shot at the Tiger's rear. This tank fired twice, but the shells did not penetrate and Wittman fired back and knocked out the Cromwell.

> Leaving Villers, Wittman joined his other tanks, replenished his ammunition and then turned his attention onto A Sqn [those vehicles stopped along the road], shooting up the entire squadron and the accompanying Rifle Brigade infantry. This was done very systematically, first knocking out the end Rifle Brigade half-track to block the road so that no one could escape, then traversing down the column hitting tanks, lorries [trucks], half-tracks, Bren carriers [small, tracked infantry carriers], etc., including a total of twenty-five armored vehicles. . . .

> Replenishing again, Wittman decided to return to Villers-Bocage but did not know that, while he had been busy with A Sqn, the situation had changed. Four Cromwells and a Firefly [a Sherman mounting the British 17-pounder gun], commanded by Lt Bill Cotton, had been despatched by B Sqn to contact A Sqn, but having found this to be impossible, had set up an ambush in the main square, together with a 6-pounder anti-tank gun. . . . Thus when Wittman, plus the other two Tigers and the Panzer IV, motored in they were heavily engaged. Lt Cotton wrote later:

>> When the Tigers were about 1,000 yd away and were broadside on to us I told 3 Troop and my gunner to fire. The firefly did the damage, but the 75s [of the Cromwells] helped and must have taken a track off one which started to circle out of control. They shot back at us, knocked the Firefly out, and its commander was hit in the head. However, at the end of a very few minutes there were three "killed" Tigers.

> The Pzkpfw IV initially escaped unscathed but was later also knocked out, by a shot up its rear. Michael Wittman and his crew escaped on foot, evaded capture and lived to fight another day.

Workers at an American tank factory admire Shermans ready for delivery. Mass production of M4s overcame German advances in guns and armor.

bombers knocked out many of the heaviest German tanks before they could encounter Allied armor. The second, and perhaps the most debilitating, reason was Germany's obsession with the gun/armor spiral. Germany's quest for bigger and better-armored fighting vehicles was keeping it from competing with the Allies in terms of quantity of tanks produced. While the German designers were investing all their time in completing the labor-intensive King Tigers and their ilk, the Americans continued to produce the easily manufactured Shermans. And the Russians, though now capable and willing to generate heavy tanks, never stopped churning out the T-34s. In essence, in the same amount of time that the Germans could create one King Tiger, the Allies could produce ten Shermans or T-34s, and the greater numbers carried the day. The fast, light Shermans fell victim to the large-caliber guns of the German defenders, but another Sherman was always there to take its place. Industrial output supplied the needed weapons for the final Allied assault—their own blitzkrieg—on the German homeland.

Chapter 2

The U-Boat: War in the Atlantic

During the Second World War, naval action in the Atlantic Ocean was predominantly characterized by submarine warfare. Although surface engagements did occur, more action took place under the waves than on top of them. Primarily, this was because Germany did not have a sizable surface fleet. Besides the *Bismarck* and its equally formidable sister ship, the *Tirpitz*, the German navy consisted only of three small battleships and a half dozen or so cruisers. Arrayed against them was the impressive British navy, which could field several battleships and a host of cruisers and smaller ships. Unable to counter the British display, the German high command chose to invest in submarines instead, pursuing a strategy that avoided engaging Britain's fleet.

The German U-boat, or *Unterseeboot* (undersea boat), had been successfully tested in the First World War. In 1914, the *U-9*, the

The U-9 *is seen on display in a German museum in 1937. This U-boat sank three British cruisers at the start of World War I.*

first German sub to see action, sank three British cruisers in less than ninety minutes. Though clearly able to contend with warships, the submarine was not designed to counter the enemy's navy. The U-boat was a predator whose prey was the merchant ships that kept England supplied with the materials it needed to fight the war. In World War I Germany unleashed its submarines on British merchant shipping to cripple its war effort, and the plan succeeded to some degree. The number of ships sunk rose from six hundred in 1915 to more than twenty-six hundred in 1917. Hundreds of thousands of tons of supplies and thousands of experienced crewmen were lost. Capitalizing on its proven track record, Germany followed the same strategy in World War II. With the fall of France in 1940 and Russia not yet in the war, Britain was an isolated nation, standing alone in its fight and dependent on foreign aid to persevere. If Germany could interrupt the flow of trade, Britain would eventually succumb. Knowing this, the German admiralty counted on the effectiveness of its undersea fleet.

The Wolf and Its Pack

The typical German U-boat in the early years of the war (the Type VIIC) was 220 feet long and carried a crew of forty-four. It was armed with fourteen torpedoes fired from four forward tubes and one aft tube, and a deck-mounted 88-mm gun. German submarines were powered by a combination of diesel and electric technology. The electric batteries needed to be recharged on the surface, which meant that the vessel could not stay submerged for more than twenty-four hours. Undersea, the submarine could run at 7.5

knots; on the surface it could run at 17 knots. Though seemingly impressive, the submarine could not outperform many of the ships it was designed to sink. On the surface, it was a target for deck guns on armed merchant ships or for faster ships that sought to ram the fragile U-boat's hull. Thus, the submarine's main asset was its ability to stay hidden, and its primary tactic was stealth.

Two Type VIIC U-boats undergo construction at a German shipyard. The Type VIIC was armed with fourteen torpedoes and an 88-mm deck gun.

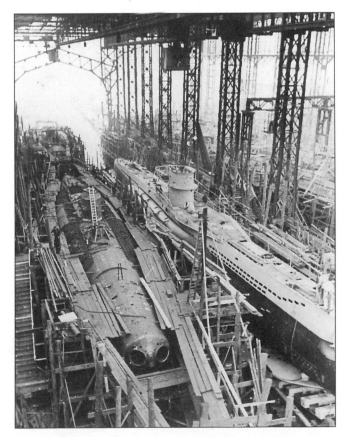

Typically, the lone submarine would first locate its victim, whether a single freighter or a convoy of ships, and then, using its speed on the surface, race ahead of the lumbering prey, partly submerge off to the side of the projected path of the enemy, and lie in wait. The maneuver was usually performed at night when subs could travel more safely on the surface. As historian Richard Humble points out, "This exploited the simple fact that a submarine's conning-tower is virtually impossible to spot at night, whereas the bulky silhouette of even a blacked-out merchantman stands out against the sky."[10] When the ship or ships passed in front of the hidden sub, the captain would order either a single torpedo or, to increase hit probability (or possibly the number of victims), an array of torpedoes to be fired.

If a torpedo hit but did not sink its target (which often was the case), the sub captain would wait until any accompanying ships abandoned the crippled vessel. (Convoys often had to abandon damaged ships, not out of heartlessness but because the success of the convoy was measured in the number of ships that reached port.) Once the damaged ship was alone, the captain would either fire off another torpedo or surface and sink the vessel using the submarine's deck gun. U-boat captains often preferred to finish off their victims on the surface because torpedoes were more valuable than the smaller and more numerous deck-gun shells. They also favored the deck gun because of the immediacy of the experience.

As submarine historian Richard Compton-Hall relates, "Torpedo attacks were often prolonged and, for most of the crew, boring and frightening by turns. . . . Gun actions, in contrast, offered instant results with little chance of retribution from puny unescorted targets."[11] On the other hand, if the target looked armed, and thus still dangerous even if damaged, the captain would opt for a second torpedo to avoid risking his ship and his crew in a surface fight. Once its victim was sinking, the submarine sometimes surfaced to pick up survivors, a chivalrous act that proved impractical given the already cramped quarters of the U-boat.

This hunting method worked well for the single submarine, but it was even more effective when U-boats prowled in packs. Coordinated, cooperative attack was the brainchild of Admiral Karl Dönitz, the commander of Germany's submarine fleet. Dönitz organized up to a dozen submarines into "wolf packs" and then sent them into areas commonly traversed by enemy shipping. His strategy was simple: One submarine would draw off any protective warships while the rest pounced on the helpless convoys. The results were devastating. On a tour in 1940, one pack of twelve U-boats claimed thirty-two enemy ships without losing a single submarine. In October of that year, the German submarines were racking up a daily total of 920 tons sunk.

The successes pleased Dönitz, who believed that Germany could bring England to its knees only if it sank 750,000 tons of cargo every month. But he needed more sub-

marines to accomplish that task. The U-boat fleet still possessed only the fifty-seven ships with which it began the war, and some of those were used for training new crews. Dönitz petitioned German chancellor Adolf Hitler many times to increase the submarine fleet. Hitler, however, wanted a fleet that could destroy warships, and, since Dönitz did not want his subs attacking ships that could fight back, the Führer was reluctant to fund the project. Only when Dönitz displayed the amount of damage the subs were doing to the British war effort did Hitler grudgingly approve an increase in the size of the U-boat fleet.

An Allied freighter sinks after having been torpedoed by a German submarine. U-boats sometimes finished off their victims with deck guns.

Protecting the Convoys

Filling the German quotas would never be easy for the U-boat crews. The British were equipped to contend with the submarine threat; they had fought U-boats in the previous war. They quickly adopted convoy tactics, sending fleets of merchant ships across the Atlantic at one time. The philosophy was to get the largest number of ships to port despite the loss of one or two to the stray submarine. Against a single sub, the strategy was sufficient; against wolf packs, the plan backfired. If one U-boat spotted a convoy, it would signal the rest of the pack (via radio) to feast on the defenseless prey. To remedy this situation, Britain offered as much protection to its convoys as it could.

Land-based aircraft shadowed convoys as they left or neared Britain. These planes were fighters or tactical bombers of the Royal Air Force, and they served a dual function. First, given their altitude, they could spot submarines at a distance that were on

or near the water's surface. Radioing the information to the convoy, the escort planes could keep the merchant ships out of a submarine's path. Second, the airplanes could actively engage the submarine. A submarine on the surface was fairly defenseless against air attack. It usually chose to dive out of harm's way, but even this took time—time an aircraft could use to cripple the submerging vessel.

Escort airplanes from England, however, were constrained by their fuel supplies, leaving convoys unprotected beyond the planes' reach. Therefore, the vast stretches of the mid-Atlantic between Britain and its primary trading partner, the United States, were the main hunting grounds for German submarines. Merchant seamen simply referred to the region as "U-boat Alley" or the "Black Gap." England needed escort capability that could stay with the convoys along their entire route, and it needed it quickly. In the first year of the war alone, submarines had claimed 438 merchant ships. They had also sunk an aircraft carrier, a battleship, five cruisers, and three destroyers. The losses would have been worse if Germany was not constrained by the low number of U-boats in service. Still, the tonnage sunk was impressive, and Britain realized it would have to try other options.

The Destroyer

Destroyers were the submarines' most formidable foe. Part of their original purpose was to engage in antisubmarine warfare. Thus the use of destroyers to combat the

Balancing Act

Submarines would rise and dive not only by pointing their noses up or down but by either allowing seawater into or pumping water out of their trim tanks, which ran along the lower spine of the ship. The submarine rarely achieved a level position in the sea because the movement of crewmen or objects on the ship always affected the trim, or pitch, of the ship. In his book *The Underwater War 1939–1945,* Richard Compton-Hall describes how interior movement was sometimes used to the sub's advantage.

> Men passing through the control room could change the fore-and-aft trim significantly and it was often a rule to ask permission before going either way. Sending men forward or aft at the rush was, in fact, an effective and rapid way of correcting a steep angle and many boats were saved in this way from plunging to the bottom under attack or when the trimming officer had simply got his sums wrong. Six men weighed the same as 100 gallons and could move much more quickly than an equivalent amount of water passing along the trim line.

A convoy sails for Britain. Destroyers equipped for antisubmarine warfare escorted the convoys through the perilous waters of the Atlantic.

having to operate in the Atlantic and the Mediterranean. Therefore its destroyers were also dispersed. They typically accompanied the larger capital ships—battleships, cruisers, and aircraft carriers—to fend off submarines that may have otherwise damaged the most valuable ships in the Royal Navy. Britain could not spare many destroyers to protect its convoys.

The Royal Navy's fortunes changed, however, by the end of 1940. America, though still not a combatant in the war, gave Britain fifty destroyers under the Lend-Lease program, a political compact that gave America the ability to supply Britain with arms without appearing to be an overt military ally. Though the English navy needed some of the vessels to recoup losses sustained by its attack fleet, most were put on convoy escort duty. These destroyers were fast and armed for antisubmarine warfare. They possessed racks of depth charges on the stern of the ship that could be easily dropped in any suspected location of an enemy U-boat. The depth charge was an explosive device timed to detonate at a preset depth. If the submarine was not struck in the explosion, the concussion could sometimes damage the ship enough to force it to surface. With the addition of destroyers, the convoys gained an offensive countermeasure to U-boats—and a degree of security.

growing U-boat threat was not novel, nor was it simply an oversight on the part of the British navy that more destroyers weren't employed early in the war. What hindered the deployment of sub-chasing destroyers was their inadequate numbers. Britain's surface fleet was large but it was stretched thin,

A geyser of salt water marks the explosion of a depth charge. These weapons were used to sink U-boats or force them to the surface.

lease its torpedoes while the destroyers sat unaware. As one captain in the Royal Navy attested, "Lacking radar, which had not yet been developed for surface warning, the escorts were helpless in the face of night attack; their defense was swamped and they could do nothing more than rescue survivors." [12] Still, the combination of destroyers and land-based aircraft patrols made convoy raiding a more dangerous task for the U-boats.

Improved Detection Devices

Perhaps the most valuable tools that aided the Allies in fighting the U-boat menace were the electronic detection devices that eventually made their way onto most Allied ships and planes. Sonar, or ASDIC as the British termed it (after its developers, the Anti-Submarine Detection Investigation Committee), provided the biggest advantage because it allowed destroyers to locate submerged U-boats. Sonar operated by sending out a sound wave in a specified direction; if the wave hit a target, it would bounce back to the receiver. Measuring how long the signal took to return indicated the depth and bearing of the enemy sub. The escorts could then swarm into the area and drop depth charges. Sonar had been developed in the years between the two world wars, but it had not been perfected or been widely available to naval vessels during the early war years. Even during its use in the war, sonar was somewhat unreliable and functioned poorly in rough seas. U-boat captains also learned how to avoid detection

But the destroyers did not eliminate the risk of attack. The Germans simply adapted to the new threat. Instead of brazenly attacking escorted convoys, the submarines would shadow the convoy until nighttime. Convoy escorts relied on visual sightings to hunt subs in the early war years, so darkness effectively rendered them blind. A U-boat could maneuver relatively close to the convoy and choose the best opportunity to re-by "hiding" behind thermal layers in the deep seas. These temperature gradients would diffuse the signal, giving the sonar operator the impression that nothing was there.

While sonar improved the chances of locating submerged submarines, radar increased the odds of finding surfaced U-boats. Radar involved the emission of radio waves toward a target and the interpretation of the resulting reflected signal. By employing radar, ships and aircraft could "spot" submarines at a great distance, giving convoys and their escorts plenty of time to react. Radar had been very successful in helping give the Royal Air Force an early-warning advantage in the air war over Britain, but it was a relatively new weapon in antisubmarine warfare. It was so advantageous, though, that, in addition to those set up to scan the skies, radar stations were located along the English coast to specifically target the surrounding waterways.

Perhaps the most unique electronic innovation employed in the Allies' antisubmarine effort was HF/DF, or high-frequency direction finder. Called "Huff-Duff" by sailors, the HF/DF was a receiver that picked up high-frequency radio waves, primarily those used by the U-boats to communicate with other submarines and the high command on shore. As a matter of protocol, sub captains sent regular reports back to the high command throughout the war. HF/DF set up along the English coast routinely picked these signals up and could send destroyers out to their point of origin. Once

the receivers were added to shipboard detection devices in 1942, the chances of spotting submarines and reaching their location quickly were greatly improved. HF/DF was one of the better kept secrets of the war; Germany never fathomed the technology and continued to have its sub captains send

The Badly Shaken

Depth charges were barrel-shaped devices filled with six hundred pounds of explosives. They were lethal if they detonated within ten or twenty feet of a U-boat's hull. If detonated at a slightly greater range, they could still shake a submarine and perhaps split its seams or disrupt some of its machinery. Regardless, the terror of being wracked by depth charges was something that most skilled crews learned to control. The crew of the *U-570*, however, was not so tolerant, as Richard Compton-Hall relates.

U-570 surfaced off Iceland in misty weather on 27 August 1941 under the nose of a patrolling Lockheed Hudson aircraft.... [The airplane] instantly straddled the target with four depth-charges which so shook the captain and crew that it was decided to surrender without a fight. Subsequent investigation showed that there was nothing in the hull damage which would have made it impossible, or even difficult, to dive the U-boat; nor would cracked battery cells have prevented escape. Supplies to the main motors, lighting and auxiliaries could have been restored very quickly and the steering and hydroplanes could have been put in hand-control; but no attempt was made to do any of these things. Although the captured crew said chlorine gas was escaping from the batteries no trace of this was found by the party sent by the Royal Navy to take the boat over. It was a case of total surprise leading to panic.

A sailor monitors a radar display aboard a destroyer. Radar was a relatively new, yet extremely effective, countermeasure to the U-boat.

their timely reports, unaware that the signals may be revealing their location. After the war, U-boat commander Peter Cremer admitted Germany's ignorance of these devices but claimed,

> We did suspect though that, somehow, the epoch of the bare eye, however good, was coming to an end and that the new era of technology, or electronics to be more precise, was upon us. War is the father of all things, and electronics developed in such a way that the U-boats were harried ever more closely, and with ever greater certainty of aim.[13]

The Escort Carrier

By 1942, the tide in U-boat warfare was turning. The improved detection devices, coupled with increased destroyer escort availability, were limiting the losses to convoys. Another weapon, the merchant carrier, had been introduced as early as 1940 in a joint effort between England and the United States. These aircraft carriers were converted merchant ship hulls that had been stripped of their superstructure and covered with wooden flight decks that held a dozen or so dive-bombers. When America entered the war in late 1941, it could turn a larger part of its production capacity to manufacturing merchant carriers. Designated CVEs or escort carriers by the U.S. Navy, these ships were first used to give extended aerial protection to convoys. Their impact was tremendous. According to the U.S. Navy, "Antisubmarine aviation was one of the most effective Allied developments of World War II, and aircraft sank or took part in half of all submarine 'kills.'"[14] The newly employed escort carriers gave convoys the ability to engage subs with aircraft in the parts of the sea beyond the reach of land-based planes. Escort carriers were so effec-

tive that Admiral Dönitz ordered U-boats to avoid attacking convoys protected by them.

Closing the Gap

Besides increasing the production of escort carriers, the U.S. contribution to the war in the Atlantic included employing B-24 Liberator bombers in the hunt for U-boats. The B-24 was a long-range bomber that increased the land-based search-and-attack radius from both the English and American coasts. In cooperation with carrier planes, nearly every region of the Atlantic was under aerial observation. And the German

Its dive-bombers having flown to airbases ashore, an escort carrier returns from convoy duty. CVEs provided aerial protection to merchant vessels.

submarine captains seemed to sense their fate. Peter Cremer recalled,

One thing was obvious: what had been so long expected had now happened. Long-distance aircraft and carriers had finally closed the so-called "Gap" in the Atlantic air surveillance. All ships on the big pond between England and America now received reconnaissance and protection from above.[15]

In 1943, the Americans began producing a new class of destroyer. Called destroyer escorts (designated DE, rather than the standard DD for a destroyer), these ships were smaller and slower than the average destroyer, but they were cheaper and quicker to build. The Allies commissioned

An American destroyer escort steams in calm seas. Instead of depth charges, many of the DEs were armed with more effective weapons known as hedgehogs.

503 of these vessels by the end of the war. The United States and Britain also began mounting a new antisubmarine device on their escort ships. These new explosive devices, called hedgehogs, were designed to replace depth charges. The hedgehog consisted of twenty-four projectiles that were flung from the fore deck of the escort. The 32-pound projectiles armed in the water and detonated only when they contacted a solid object. The hedgehog had an advantage over the depth charge because depth charges exploded regardless of whether they struck an object. The explosion often interfered with the sonar contact established with the target, sometimes allowing the sub to escape in the confusion. If the hedgehog didn't find its target, it would not explode until it hit the bottom of the sea, too far down to disrupt the sonar's signal. Flung in a wide array, the hedgehog projectiles could cover a large area, almost ensuring that any sub picked up on sonar would be struck with at least one explosive.

The new methods of locating and destroying the subs turned the Allies' defensive war of protecting convoys into an offensive war of U-boat hunting. Despite objections from the British who wished to keep their vital supply lines safe, the Allies eventually formed hunter-killer groups in June 1943, removing some escort ships from their convoy duties. These groups, made up of one CVE and up to four destroyer escorts, went out in search of the U-boats. The active pursuit of submarines, coupled with the advances in technology and escort patterns, cut British shipping losses in 1943 by 65 percent. The following year, losses dropped another 65 percent, leaving the German U-boats to claim only two hundred vessels sunk.

The Last Efforts

The Germans were not idle in trying to improve their deteriorating situation. Each year saw the development of several new models of U-boats, each increasing speed and underwater endurance. In a conference in January 1944, Admiral Dönitz proclaimed, "The submarine weapon has not been broken by the setbacks of 1943. On the contrary, it has become stronger. In 1944, which will be a successful but a hard year, we shall smash Britain's supply line with a new submarine weapon."[16] In the winter of that year, the Germans had commissioned the Type XXI submarine, which had three times the power of the Type VIIC and could carry up to twenty-three torpedoes. The Type XXI subs were 250 feet long and could run submerged at an incredible seventeen knots. They could dive to a depth of 850 feet (nearly twice the operating depth of any other submarine) and stay submerged for up to four days while traveling at slow speeds. Their hull was coated with rubber, which deflected radar and sonar signals. The Type XXI U-boats were also equipped with a revolutionary device—the snorkel— that allowed them to recharge their batteries without surfacing. The snorkel was a tube that ran to the surface and brought in air while allowing the sub's engines to vent

Life Underwater

Service in the U-boat fleet was demanding. Quarters were cramped, and the stench of human perspiration was as pervasive as that of oil and fuel. The environment was dark and dismal, and fresh air and light arrived only when the ship surfaced in the daytime, a period when it was most vulnerable to attack. In a speech given at a German naval officers convention in 1943, sub captain Wolfgang Lueth described his experience and his duties aboard the *U-181*. Historian Richard Compton-Hall provides an excerpt of that speech in *The Underwater War 1939–1945*.

It is my job as a submarine commander to sink ships. To do this I need a co-operative crew so that everything clicks. . . . Life aboard is monotonous for long periods. For many long weeks one must be able to bear failures, and when depth charges are added life becomes a war of nerves. . . . Life aboard a submarine is unnatural and unhealthy . . . there is no constant change between day and night for the lights have to burn all the time. . . . The captain must attempt to compensate for these disadvantages as far as possible. . . . There is no regular time for sleeping, since most of the fighting is done at night. Continuous responsibility rests with the captain for weeks and he must be alert at all times.

exhaust. This allowed subs to continually operate while remaining underwater.

Britain rightly feared the implementation of such a submarine. The British admiralty believed that Germany could field sixty of the Type XXI subs by January 1945 and another thirty by spring. But the prediction did not come true. The Allies had already landed in Europe and spread through France, the home of many of the submarine bases. The German engineers were working against the advancing Allied ground troops and a lack of supplies because of the continuing Allied air campaign. They were able to put only two Type XXI subs in service in January. Production did continue, though; 140 Type XXI subs were completed by the end of the war, yet only a few of those were in active service. In fact, in the early winter months of 1945, German U-boats never sank more than 65,000 tons of shipping in any month. It was a far cry from Dönitz's estimation of the 750,000 tons per month that Germany would need to win the war.

As the war in Europe was drawing to a close, Admiral Dönitz realized the U-boat fleet was not going to change Germany's fortunes. He began rerouting supplies to protect the civilian populations on the eastern front from the oncoming Russian juggernaut. In the final months, the Nazi government was plagued with coup attempts, and Hitler turned to Dönitz to take over the reins of state. Though the admiral and the Führer had disagreed many times over the importance of U-boats, Hitler trusted Dönitz's loyalty. It was Dönitz who accepted the terms for Germany's surrender in May 1945, and immediately thereafter his once proud fleet of 140 U-boats were scuttled or were turned over to the Allies. The U-boat war had ended.

Chapter 3

Flattops: The Carrier War in the Pacific

In the early morning of December 7, 1941, 353 Japanese dive-bombers, torpedo bombers, and fighter aircraft, flying in two waves, surprised a large part of America's Pacific fleet in port at the Pearl Harbor naval base in the Hawaiian Islands. The planes had been detected on radar several miles out from the base, but they were mistaken for friendly aircraft. At that time, the United States was not involved in World War II, and no one had suspected that a potential enemy could come within striking distance of American shores without some advanced warning—at least a declaration of war. The Japanese fleet was counting on surprise. Vice Admiral Chuichi Nagumo knew that the American fleet was formidable, and he did not want to risk engaging it in a surface action. He had only two battleships and three cruisers, while the U.S. Navy had eight battleships

at hand. He had to eliminate the U.S. fleet without endangering his smaller force, so he relied on his most powerful asset—his six aircraft carriers.

Nagumo's now-legendary raid was in some respects a success. Four U.S. battleships sank or capsized; one was badly damaged and lay aground; the other three were

Surrounded by burning fuel oil, the battleship USS California *sinks during the Japanese attack on Pearl Harbor.*

damaged but still afloat. Three light cruisers, three destroyers, and some minor vessels were also damaged, as well as 350 aircraft. A total of 2,403 men had been killed and another 1,178 injured. But the Japanese had lost an important opportunity—both by choice and by chance. The port installations at Pearl Harbor, including the fuel-storage depots and the repair facilities, were not targeted by the bombers and thus were undamaged. More important, the Japanese failed to catch any American aircraft carriers in port. The four U.S. carriers were at sea when the attack came and were spared the fate of the battleships. Military historian Clark G. Reynolds called the attack ill conceived, claiming, "It bought precious little time for the Japanese. It enraged the Americans and unified them in their quest for revenge. And it forced the U.S. Navy, deprived of its battleships, to rely on the very weapon Japan had used to destroy them—the aircraft carrier."[17]

The Birth of the Flattop

Although it came to symbolize the naval war in the Pacific, the concept of the aircraft carrier was presented in 1909 at an air show in France. After witnessing the air show feats and thrills, two officers of the U.S. and British navies presented to their respective governments the idea that airplanes could

A British biplane returns to the aircraft carrier Illustrious *after striking the Italian fleet in Taranto Harbor.*

be used offensively in naval combat. In 1910, the Americans were the first to launch a plane from a ship, but in this case the ship was a cruiser with a ramp attached to the bow. Britain took the lead in naval air experiments, making such modifications to a few warships during the First World War. But it wasn't until the postwar years that Britain, the United States, and Japan (another growing naval power) built true "flattops," ships with operational flight decks that ran from end to end of the ship, depriving the vessels of large-caliber guns but giving them the ability to launch and retrieve aircraft.

The power of the new carriers was first demonstrated in World War II when a dozen British biplanes launched from the aircraft carrier *Illustrious* attacked the Italian fleet in Taranto Harbor on November 11, 1940. The rather outdated aircraft, braving steady antiaircraft fire, managed to drop bombs and launch torpedoes at the anchored ships. A second squadron of nine planes from the *Illustrious* followed them. In total, the British pilots disabled three battleships, a cruiser, and two destroyers—half of the entire Italian navy—while suffering the loss of only two planes. The future of naval warfare was forever changed.

The Modern Aircraft Carrier

The *Illustrious* was the world's first fully armored carrier with a steel flight deck. In that respect, it was unlike the Japanese and American carriers that fought in the Pacific War. The Japanese had eight carriers at the outset of the war. They ranged from the massive *Akagi* and *Kaga* built in the 1920s and displacing more than forty thousand tons (the weight of a ship is given by the amount of water it displaces when afloat), to the faster, more modern attack carriers *Shokaku* and *Zuikaku* displacing thirty thousand tons, to the diminutive *Ryujo* displacing a mere fourteen thousand tons. These ships had wooden decks and little superstructure, both innovations to make them lighter and able to carry more planes. Altogether, the Japanese carrier fleet could hold more than five hundred aircraft, including fighters, bombers, and torpedo bombers. The air arm of the Imperial Navy was powerful, and it had practiced carrier takeoffs and landings for many years before the war. Its pilots were experienced, having participated in operations against China in the 1930s.

However, the Japanese knew that the U.S. Navy was also strong. Besides its impressive fleet of battleships, the U.S. Navy had four of its seven main aircraft carriers assigned to the Pacific, and the USS *Yorktown* would be transferred from the Atlantic fleet at the outbreak of war. The medium-sized *Yorktown*, *Hornet*, and *Enterprise* were built in the 1930s and could travel up to thirty-three knots with an average twenty-six-thousand ton displacement. Each could field eighty-one airplanes. The *Lexington* and *Saratoga* were older but larger carriers displacing forty-seven thousand tons. They could speed at thirty-four knots and carry up to ninety aircraft. Despite their low number, all of the American ships had a distinct

The U.S. aircraft carriers USS Lexington *(top)* and USS Yorktown *(right)*.

advantage over their Japanese counterparts. The Americans possessed shipboard radar, which allowed their task forces to detect enemy aircraft as they approached, giving the defenders time to prepare. The Japanese had failed to develop this technology for its fleet. With their five vessels and their one tactical advantage, the Americans would sail against an enemy that had nearly twice as many carriers in its fleet, a fact that worried commanders in the Pacific Theater.

Japan's Early Victories

After the success at Pearl Harbor, the Japanese followed with a series of more important victories. Imperial marines had landed at strategic locations all over Indochina. The Philippine Islands were invaded in December, and American troops stationed there were eventually overwhelmed. Thailand, Burma, and the Malay Peninsula were taken from British hands; the Dutch East Indies was taken from the Netherlands. By spring 1942, much of New Guinea had fallen and the Japanese expansion covered nearly the entire western rim of the Pacific Ocean. The land grab had one aim: to provide Japan with valuable resources, since the island nation was dependent on imports to maintain its war effort. Knowing that American industry would eventually outdo Japan's production, the Japanese war ministers needed to acquire resources and deliver a decisive blow to the United States. Admiral Isoroku Yamamoto, the head of the Japanese navy, understood this when he told his prime minister, "I guarantee to put up a tough fight for the first six months, but I have absolutely no confidence as to what might happen if [the war] went on for two or three years." [18]

Although the attack on Pearl Harbor did not turn out to be the decisive blow, the Allies were suffering at sea as much as they had on land. Three days after Pearl Harbor, Japanese land-based aircraft sank two British battleships, thus ending Britain's naval influence in the area and leaving America the main seagoing combatant. In January, a Japanese submarine crippled the USS *Saratoga*, forcing it into repairs for some time. The Americans now had only four carriers at sea. The Japanese, on the other hand, had added two more small carriers to their fleet, bringing their total carrier strength up to ten.

Despite so many setbacks, the Americans were still audacious. In April 1942, sixteen B-25 medium-range bombers under the command of Colonel James Doolittle were launched from the deck of the USS *Hornet* and bombed Tokyo. Doolittle's raid was a complete surprise, though the military effect was negli-

gible. As historian Harry A. Gailey writes, "Physical damage from the bombing was insignificant, and most of the planes crash-landed in China. . . . The psychological impact of the Doolittle raid was another thing entirely." [19] The Japanese believed they had control of the Pacific and felt that their homeland was safe from attack. The Americans proved them wrong, and showed that they were far from beaten.

Japanese troops celebrate the capture of the Philippine Islands. By the spring of 1942, Japan had conquered nearly all of the western Pacific.

Coral Sea

Despite the American bravado, Japan still dominated the Pacific. Following victories in New Guinea, Japan's next logical step was to move into the Coral Sea between New Guinea and Australia and grab the Solomon Islands. American intelligence discerned the logic and sent Rear Admiral Frank Fletcher and Task Force 17 into the region in May 1942. With Task Force 17 were the carriers *Lexington* and *Yorktown*. Opposing them was a sizable Japanese fleet that included the carriers *Shokaku* and *Zuikaku*, veterans of the Pearl Harbor attack, and a landing force of Imperial marines. The Americans lost the opening rounds; the Japanese marines landed on the island of

Bound for Tokyo, a B-25 bomber takes off from the USS Hornet. *The Doolittle raid proved that the Japanese were not invulnerable to attack.*

Tulagi unopposed on May 4. The following days were spent in wild goose chases as the two navies tried but failed to locate each other's main fleet. On May 7, however, dive-bombers from the *Lexington* and *Yorktown* spotted the Japanese light carrier *Shoho*. Within ten minutes, the *Shoho* was burning and sinking—a record that was not repeated throughout the rest of the war.

On May 8, the main bout occurred. Fletcher and his counterpart, Admiral Takagi, found each other and sent squadrons of planes into the air. The air forces were evenly matched; the Japanese had 121 aircraft, the Americans had 122. But at sea, the Japanese had a decided advantage—not in number of ships but in the form of a protective layer of overcast that hid the Japanese carriers. Missing the rain-shrouded *Zuikaku* completely, American bombers concentrated on the *Shokaku*. Three bombs found their mark, one bending the flight deck so much that the carrier could no longer launch planes. The Americans fared worse. The *Yorktown* took two bomb hits, and the *Lexington* was hit twice by both bombs and torpedoes. By the end of the encounter, the *Lexington* was listing and on fire. Though damage control should have been able to contend with the fires, two internal explosions forced the crew to abandon ship. An American destroyer torpedoed the flame-engulfed wreck, sending it to the bottom, where it could not be salvaged by the Japanese. "The first clash between the two air arms was over," writes British naval historian Donald Macintyre. "Exaggerated claims by aviators on either side were inevitable; each side believed itself the victor."[20] The Japanese had taken one of the valuable American carriers out of the war, but the Americans had frightened the Japanese enough to cease further amphibious operations in the area. In addition, the Japanese were forced to retire the *Shokaku* for a period of repairs, and the *Zuikaku* had to be withdrawn to have its lost planes replaced.

Already set aflame by a previous hit, the Japanese carrier Shoho *is struck by a bomb during the Battle of the Coral Sea.*

The Aircraft

The complement of aircraft aboard the *Zuikaku*—as aboard most Japanese carriers in the early years of the Pacific conflict—included the Nakajima B5N2 Type 97 bomber (code-named "Kate" by the Allies). Although designated a bomber, the Kate served as a torpedo plane, flying just above the water and perpendicular to the flank of an enemy ship before dropping its torpedo from several hundred feet away. The Aichi D3A1 Type 99 bomber (code-named "Val") filled the role of the primary Japanese dive-bomber. The Val could travel only 240 mph, but it was so light and maneuverable that it was often used as a fighter plane. The Zero, or Mitsubishi A6M Type O, was the standard Japanese fighter plane, however. One of the fastest and most agile planes of the war, the Zero could fly at an impressive 330 mph. To achieve this, the Zero, like most Japanese planes, sacrificed armor plating and heavy self-sealing fuel tanks (fuel tanks that would reseal if punctured by a bullet).

American engineers believed that both armor and self-sealing fuel tanks were essential components; thus, U.S. planes tended to be heavier and slower than the Japanese models. The Douglas TBD-1 Devastator torpedo bomber had all-metal construction and could reach a top speed of only 206 mph (slow compared with the Kate's 235 mph). The armored Grumman F4F-4 Wildcat fighter was clumsy when compared with the Zero, and it did not have the range of the enemy aircraft (770 miles compared with the Zero's 1,930 miles). But the emphasis on armor made the American planes more rugged. The Douglas SBD-3 Dauntless dive-bomber could take tremendous punishment and still return to its carrier's flight deck. The Dauntless was also one of the few American planes that was comparable, if not superior, to its Japanese counterpart. It could attain a maximum speed of 250 mph and had a longer range and heavier payload than the Japanese Val. The Dauntless proved to be one of the best American planes, one that helped turn the tide in the Pacific War.

During the first months of the war, the Mitsubishi A6M Zero fighter was faster and more maneuverable than American warplanes.

Midway

The Battle of the Coral Sea was the first contest between opposing aircraft carriers. As Donald Macintyre notes, the conflict was significant because it "introduced the new face of naval warfare in which battles were won or lost without the opposing fleets ever coming within sight of one another."[21] This new type of warfare would continue to shape the character of the Pacific War, perhaps most famously at the Battle of Midway.

Roughly a month after the Battle of the Coral Sea, the Japanese intended to bring a carrier strike force in range of Midway Island, a tiny dot in the Pacific that gave the Americans a base of operations closer to the theater of war than the Hawaiian Islands. Besides being a staging point for the Americans, Midway was also a strategic air base, allowing long-range bombers to strike targets far away. Furthermore, seizing Midway would give the Japanese a base only eleven hundred miles from Hawaiian shores, a thought repellent to the Americans.

With the *Shokaku* and *Zuikaku* temporarily withdrawn, Admiral Yamamoto planned to have his remaining carriers swamp Midway's air defenses one day and then have a landing force storm ashore the next. He hoped that the Americans would respond by bringing their carriers into the battle to rescue the island, allowing the Japanese—who would then have a land-based airstrip as well as carriers—to elimi-

A Douglas SBD-3 Dauntless dive-bomber flies over an island in the Pacific. The Duuntless was one of the best American planes of World War II.

nate the threat with their superior airpower. Yamamoto's plan, however, had two fatal flaws. First, he believed that the USS *Yorktown* had been too badly damaged in the Coral Sea to still be active. He assumed that his chosen four carriers—*Akagi, Kaga, Soryu,* and *Hiryu*—would be facing only the *Enterprise* and the *Hornet*. In fact, the *Yorktown* had been patched up in two days at Pearl Harbor and was speeding to the sea around Midway. Second, Yamamoto's scheme relied on secrecy, but U.S. code breakers had deciphered his instructions and general battle plans as they were transmitted to the fleet. U.S. admiral Chester Nimitz was prepared.

The battle opened on June 4 when a scout plane from the island caught sight of two Japanese carriers two hundred miles

An oil tank burns on Midway after the Japanese air raid. While the island took a beating, American guns shot down a third of the attacking planes.

west of Midway. The carriers—*Kaga* and *Akagi*—had just launched more than one hundred planes at the island. The island's radar had picked up the approaching aircraft and available defending planes were put into the skies. But the twenty-seven American aircraft were no match; twenty-three were either shot down or badly damaged. The American bomber and torpedo planes that were stationed on Midway had been scrambled when the radar had picked up the incoming squadrons, and they were sent at the Japanese carriers without fighter escort. When the Japanese overcame the defending planes, the island took a pounding. A third of the attacking aircraft, however, were destroyed by antiaircraft fire. This was a terrible loss to the Japanese, who were expecting complete surprise to carry the day.

Realizing that the Japanese aircraft were off the decks of the two found carriers, Admiral Nimitz ordered the *Enterprise* and *Hornet* to launch an attack. Twenty-nine Devastators, sixty-seven Dauntlesses, and twenty Wildcats were sent at the Japanese. (Thirty-six fighters were left behind to protect the American carriers.) Before this attack group could reach the Japanese fleet, however, the few unprotected planes from Midway reached the Japanese fleet and staged a desperate strike. Four B-26s armed with torpedoes and six Devastators made their run, but the antiaircraft from the ships was thick. Zero fighters flying protective "cap" (combat air patrol) around the carriers also jumped on the tiny American force, cutting down seven of the attackers. Two B-26s and one Devastator limped back to Midway; none of the dropped torpedoes had found its mark.

Admiral Nagumo, in charge of the Japanese carrier fleet, believed correctly that the attacking force had come from Midway, and he concluded that the island would need another aerial pounding. He had several torpedo bombers on deck that were ready to launch at any enemy carrier force in the area, but needing the aircraft for this second attack, he ordered the planes below deck to be rearmed with bombs suitable for attacking the island. A second wave of American planes from Midway arrived soon after Nagumo made the decision to rearm. Although this force had a total strength of forty-two planes, they were easily dispatched or fended off by the protecting Zeros. To further complicate matters, a Japanese scout plane had just detected an American fleet that seemed to include a carrier. Nagumo rescinded his last order and had his planes rearmed again with their original ordnance. He was also saddled with the job of receiving his planes returning from the attack on Midway, meaning that he would have to wait longer before launching his attack against the sighted American carrier.

While Nagumo was managing all these time-consuming tasks, two torpedo squadrons and two fighter squadrons from the *Hornet* and *Enterprise* reached the Japanese carriers. The fighters were flying quite a bit higher than the Devastators and had consequently lost touch with their charges. Upon arrival, the fifteen unprotected torpedo planes from the *Hornet* and ten from the *Enterprise* were shot down without scoring a hit. Another squadron, this time from the *Yorktown*, which had been late to launch its planes, arrived twenty minutes later. Twelve Devastators, protected by six Wildcats, moved in, but they were destroyed or fended off by the Zeros. The Americans had now attacked the Japanese with ninety-three bombers and torpedo planes, none of which had damaged a single Japanese vessel.

Nagumo began his own launching operations as the last of the *Yorktown*'s planes were being dealt with. But when the first plane rolled down the flight deck, a lookout spotted more incoming planes. This time four squadrons of Dauntless dive-bombers from the *Enterprise* and *Yorktown* had finally reached their mark. And since the Zeros flying cap were still tangling with the remaining Devastators and Wildcats, they were unopposed. The *Enterprise* squadrons went in. As former Dauntless pilot Harold L. Buell notes, "It was an attack of unbelievable quickness, completeness, and luck. The Japanese carrier leaders literally did not know what hit them."[22] Four bombs struck the *Kaga* as its planes were preparing for takeoff. Fuel and ordnance went up in flames. The *Akagi* suffered a similar fate; one bomb hit the elevators used to bring the planes up from below deck, and two bombs hit the flight deck, where a large red circle representing the Japanese Rising Sun flag

Swatting at Ships

During the Second World War, Harold L. Buell was a Dauntless dive-bomber pilot aboard the USS *Enterprise*. In his book *Dauntless Helldivers*, he describes the difficulty of hitting a maneuvering warship with a bomb dropped from a fast-moving plane.

The real test of a naval dive-bomber was hitting a moving target—a ship at sea going full speed and maneuvering. Different enemy ships posed relatively more difficult targets. Aircraft carriers were the largest and most vulnerable warship targets, followed by battleships, cruisers, and destroyers in that order. Transport ships were the easiest to attack and hit, partly due to less speed of movement and less AA [antiaircraft] fire. This latter factor [AA fire] became a deterrent to a hit on a warship because it was heavier from these ships than from a support vessel.

Those who insist that AA fire was no factor in causing bomb misses must not have dived very much on warships in a task force formation. It required mental discipline, as well as courage, for a dive-bomber pilot to ignore heavy fire and press home his attack while also selecting the precise point at which it was necessary to aim his bomb in order to secure a hit. With the ship moving at full speed and maneuvering wildly, it took the same qualities of marksmanship as a sharpshooter to put a shot into a target consistently.

When one considers the heterogeneous variables at work in a typical dive-bomber attack upon a moving target, it was amazing that hits occurred at all. (And sometimes they didn't!) Attacking a gyrating ship with great maneuverability (a destroyer, for example) has been compared to trying to hit a cockroach racing across a kitchen floor with a small flyswatter.

At Midway, Dauntless dive-bombers loom over a burning Japanese aircraft carrier.

was painted. Mike Micheel, a dive-bomber pilot, recalled, "How nice it was to have a big red dot in the center of the flight deck for an aiming point!"[23] Meanwhile, the *Yorktown* squadrons pursued the *Soryu*. Three bombs found their mark, igniting ordnance and destroying part of the flight deck. The *Enterprise* dive-bomber squadrons had lost fourteen of thirty planes; the *Yorktown* dive-bomber squadrons had escaped unscathed. Three of four Japanese carriers were burning.

The Japanese were quick to respond. Following the *Yorktown*'s bombers home, planes from the *Hiryu*, lying a bit to the north of the other carriers, attacked. *Yorktown*'s defending Wildcats and its antiaircraft claimed thirteen of eighteen Val dive-bombers. The five that got through, however, scored three hits. The flight deck caught on fire, and two bombs penetrated below deck, putting out some of the ship's boilers. Slowed significantly but with fires eventually under control, the *Yorktown* refueled its protective fighters. But before they could launch, a torpedo plane squadron from the *Hiryu* approached from the horizon. Most of these Kates were shot down, but five launched their torpedoes. Two struck the ship, and the lower decks on the port side began filling with water. The *Yorktown* began to list, and the captain, fearing the ship would capsize, ordered it abandoned.

As a destroyer stands by, the USS Yorktown *lists to port after being hit by bombs and torpedoes. Efforts to save the ship were futile.*

The *Hiryu*'s victory was short-lived. An American scout plane found the remaining carrier, and the *Enterprise* launched twenty-four Dauntlesses to attack. Like the other carriers, the *Hiryu* was caught with planes on its deck, awaiting a twilight launch. Four bombs ripped into the neat rows of parked planes. Now all the Japanese carriers were on fire. The *Soryu* and *Kaga* would perish under the water that night. The *Hiryu* would follow the next morning, a few hours after the *Akagi*, still burning, was scuttled by its crew. Upon hearing the news, Yamamoto toyed with the idea of calling in his remaining small carriers to carry on the fight. But instead he issued an order on June 5 that declared that the Midway operation was canceled. His only comfort came when a Japanese submarine reported that it had found and fired two torpedoes into the listing *Yorktown,* which American salvage crews were trying to stabilize. The carrier sank two days later after further repair efforts proved useless.

The Solomon Sea

On June 6 the USS *Saratoga* completed its repairs and sailed into Pearl Harbor. Four days later the carrier *Wasp* was transferred into the Pacific from the Mediterranean. With four carriers against the Japanese *Zuikaku, Shokaku,* and smaller flattops, the Americans went on the offensive. Midway had proven to be the turning point of the Pacific War.

In the summer of 1942, three of the American carriers participated in the initial stages of reclaiming the Solomon Islands. Guadalcanal and Tulagi were the first to be invaded, but the Japanese air and ground forces put up stiff resistance. The fight was the first time that Japanese land-based pilots had encountered the now-experienced American carrier airmen. Forty-two Japanese planes were knocked out of the skies during three days of defensive sorties. Despite the successes in the air, Admiral Fletcher, in charge of the carrier group, withdrew. He feared further contact would jeopardize the flattops' safety.

Admiral Yamamoto was eager to have these prizes, so he brought his remaining fleet into the Solomon Sea. He planned to lure the American carriers into a trap by using his light carrier *Ryujo* as bait. He hoped that the American carriers would spot the *Ryujo* and launch an attack, thus giving away their position and leaving them open for attack by planes from the *Shokaku* and *Zuikaku.* Yamamoto's plan worked. Fletcher launched from the *Enterprise* and *Saratoga* (he had sent the *Wasp* away to be refueled). The *Ryujo* succumbed to dive-bomb attacks in which not a single U.S. plane was lost. But the *Shokaku* and *Zuikaku,* waiting nearby, had launched too. The attacking Vals, covered by Zero fighters, penetrated the American cap above the *Enterprise*'s task force. Three bombs hit its decks, but the damage was manageable. After recovering its planes, it was sent back to Pearl Harbor for repairs.

A bomb explodes on the flight deck of the USS Enterprise. *The ship survived the blow and was able to recover its planes.*

The fight for the Solomon Sea resulted in an unequal trade; the tiny *Ryujo* was worth sacrificing for the time that the *Enterprise* would be laid up in port.

Two other, more pressing disasters quickly followed for the U.S. carrier fleet. This time the Japanese threat came from beneath the ocean rather than from the skies. On August 31, a Japanese submarine damaged the *Saratoga*, sending it for repairs in a naval base near the Fiji Islands. And on September 15, the *Wasp* was struck by submarine torpedoes and damaged enough that it had to be evacuated and sunk. The *Hornet* was now alone in the Pacific against the *Shokaku*, *Zuikaku*, and three light carriers. The Japanese, however, made nothing of the advantage. Instead they worked out a plan to coordinate ground and sea forces in an attempt to retake Henderson Airfield on Guadalcanal. The plan failed, and the Japanese soldiers were repulsed.

Santa Cruz

The maneuver gave the Americans much-needed time. On October 24, the *Enterprise* finished its repairs and rejoined the *Hornet*. The odds were still against them, but they had improved. When two scout planes from the *Enterprise* located Nagumo's carriers near the Santa Cruz Islands, the scout planes—Dauntless dive-bombers—tried to strike but were chased away. Two more scout bombers had better luck. Evading the Japanese Zeros, the two planes dropped their bombs and crippled the light carrier *Zuiho*. *Shokaku* and *Zuikaku*, however, had al-

ready launched their planes. Finding the *Hornet*, the Japanese bombers attacked. Weaving through antiaircraft and Wildcat defenders, the Japanese pilots put one bomb and two torpedoes into the carrier. Another Japanese pilot, whose plane was badly damaged but still carrying its bombs, crashed into and through the *Hornet*'s deck. The ship lay dead in the water, but its fifty-four attack planes had already launched against the Japanese carriers.

Joined by a force from the *Enterprise*, the *Hornet*'s planes eventually found the *Shokaku*. As the Dauntlesses came in, a pair of American airmen who were shot down near the fight reported what they saw while afloat in a rubber life raft. One of the two, Lieutenant Commander William J. Widhelm, said the dive-bombers "swooped in low and laid their eggs in a line, full length along the deck. It was like blasting a ditch to drain a swamp."[24] *Shokaku*, though not sunk, was out of commission for nine months. A second wave of *Shokaku*'s planes, however, was still airborne. They found the *Enterprise* and planted two bombs on the deck. Damaged, the ship headed for repairs. The *Hornet* meanwhile had already been ordered abandoned. American destroyers tried to sink the listing ship but failed. Later, two Japanese destroyers who found the floating hulk succeeded. The Battle of Santa Cruz was over. The Americans had held off the Japanese effort to regain control of Guadalcanal, but they had done so at the price of having no operational carriers in the Pacific for the following two weeks.

The New Warriors

The dearth of operational carriers was distressing for the Americans, but fortune was in their favor. The Japanese had not lost as many carriers, but they had lost many carrier planes. Even though they now had the time to rebuild, they lacked the production capability and the resources. The Japanese prophecy was coming true; as 1943 loomed, American production was outpacing the Japanese. Thirty-three new carriers—nine *Independence*-class carriers built on cruiser hulls and twenty-four *Essex*-class carriers— were being constructed in U.S. shipyards. The *Essex*-class ships were more maneuverable and better defended (with both armor and antiaircraft weapons) than previous models. America was also developing escort carriers, tiny flattops built on merchantman hulls, to perform antisubmarine duties in the Atlantic as well as assist with forthcoming landing operations on Japanese-held islands in the Pacific.

Besides new carriers, the United States was implementing new aircraft. The Curtiss SB2C Helldiver dive-bomber would supplement the Dauntless, and the Chance Vought F4U Corsair and Grumman F6F Hellcat fighters would not only replace the outdated Wildcat but also outperform the fearsome Zero. As aviation historian David C. Cooke attests, "By 1943, the newer Allied airplanes were able to run rings around the once-deadly enemy, shooting it down in wholesale numbers."[25] And while Japan struggled to make up its plane

A Grumman F6F Hellcat waits for the takeoff signal (top) as a Curtiss SB2C Helldiver circles another carrier before landing (right). Japanese aircraft were no match for newer American warplanes.

losses, American aircraft factories sent nearly 100,000 new planes to the Pacific.

With the new ships arriving in late 1943, the Americans began their famous "island hopping" attacks. Seizing one island through combined operations, including carrier support, American marines would immediately begin building or clearing airstrips to help give more firepower when invading the next island. The Japanese tried to thwart the attacks with their land-based planes, but the Hellcats from the escort carriers were superior. The Japanese were losing more and more valuable aircraft and pilots, whereas the Americans, by mid-November, had eleven aircraft carriers filled with planes. Outside of Guadalcanal and Tulagi in the South Pacific, Makin, Tarawa, Kwajalein, Majuro, and Eniwetok were the first islands to be retaken in the Central Pacific. At Eniwetok, the Japanese lost more than 250 land-based aircraft and forty-one ships to American carrier planes. It was the largest carrier action in the war.

The remaining Japanese carriers were not idle, but they were not a major threat. Their role was being taken over by the land-based aircraft now that America was bringing the battle to the islands. Their planes were also no match for the American fighters. Sorties that went up were inevitably shot down. In the Mariana Islands, 350 Japanese airplanes were shot down, compared with 30 American planes. Also in the battle for the Marianas, the newest Japanese carrier, *Taiho*, was sunk, as was the newly refurbished *Shokaku*. The *Zuikaku* and two light carriers were heavily damaged when they tried to flee the fight.

The Japanese were losing the war in the Pacific. Their army was on the defensive, their carrier fleet was almost nonexistent, their surface fleet of battleships and cruisers—though impressive—was trying to stay out of the range of the American carriers, and their air force was unable to cope with the better American planes. Desperation, however, turned to fanaticism. A new threat to American warships, especially carriers, appeared in the skies on October 25, 1944. Five Japanese Zeros flew at a group of six escort carriers in Leyte Gulf off the Philippines. Normally five fighter planes would not be a major concern for a fleet of warships with plenty of antiaircraft to fend them off. In this case, the Japanese were not frightened. They plunged through the flak, taking hits seemingly without regard for their own survival. They were the first "kamikaze," Japanese pilots who attempted to intentionally crash their planes into enemy ships. Two of the Zero fighters penetrated the antiaircraft fire and struck two separate escort carriers. One punched through the deck of the *St. Lo* and ignited fuel and ordnance. The ship erupted and, within a half-hour, sank.

The appearance of the kamikaze heralded the future of the Pacific naval war. The Japanese, unable to contend with the more numerous and more powerful American navy and air force, would simply hurl their pilots at the enemy as living bombs, hoping to do as much damage as possible in a vain effort to show their dedication and their ferocity. It was a fear tactic, and it was effective in many ways. The Americans had no countermeasure other than trying to divert the kamikaze plane's course by antiaircraft fire or by interceptor planes. With squadrons of the remaining Japanese planes coming in all at once, a good percentage always got through the defenses. In fact, roughly 25 percent of kamikaze pilots scored hits on U.S. ships.

The Philippine Sea and the End

With U.S. carriers within range of the Philippines and poised to support an amphibious assault, the Japanese were running out of effective stratagems. In an effort to draw off the American carriers and allow the relatively strong Japanese battleships to move in and intercept any force heading toward the Philippine shores, the Japanese fleet commander Jisaburo Ozawa (who had replaced Nagumo) offered his remaining carriers as bait. On October 23, with the *Zuikaku* carrying the admiral's flag, Ozawa steered away from the islands while sending out long messages that he hoped would attract the enemy carriers. The plan worked too well. By the end of the day, the carriers *Zuikaku*, *Chitose*, *Zuiho*, and *Chiyoda* were sunk. Unfortunately, one of the battleships that was in-

Trailing flames, a kamikaze misses an escort carrier. Roughly 25 percent of kamikaze pilots did succeed in hitting their targets.

tended to evade the American carriers in this decoy maneuver was also sunk. All told in the Battle of Leyte Gulf, the Japanese lost four carriers, three battleships, nine cruisers, and eight destroyers. The United States had suffered the loss of the *St. Lo* and the escort carrier *Gambier Bay* to attack (the *Gambier Bay* was sunk by Japanese naval gunfire).

The carrier *Princeton* was struck by a kamikaze pilot and was damaged so badly that the ship was scuttled.

In the following months, kamikaze pilots struck more U.S. carriers. Japanese desperation was causing American frustration. In response, the U.S. carriers developed a strategy in which three "orbits" of planes would protect the ships. The farthest would actively attack Japanese airstrips, hoping to cut down on enemy aircraft and disrupt concerted launches. The middle orbit would patrol the seas around the carrier, and the final orbit would remain on the flight deck, ready for immediate launch in response to attack. The strategy was a success: No carriers were damaged by kamikazes during the invasion of the Philippines.

The kamikaze threat, however, didn't end after the taking of the Philippines. When the invasion of the "stepping-stone"

Carriers in Combat

During the Battle of Samar (part of the Leyte Gulf operations), several American escort carriers and a handful of destroyers ran into a large part of Japan's fleet composed of battleships and heavy cruisers. The aircraft carriers (as well as the destroyers that escorted them) were not designed for surface engagements, and thus the appearance of cruisers with 8-inch guns startled the Americans. In his account of the action, Samuel Eliot Morison describes the bravado and black humor the outgunned Americans exhibited as they were compelled to defend against the oncoming threat.

The battle reached a crisis when [Japanese admiral] Kurita's four remaining heavy cruisers *Chikuma*, *Tone*, *Haguro* and *Chokai*, more enterprising than his battlewagons, pulled ahead on the port quarter of the [American] carriers and closed range. *Chikuma* began a steady pounding of *Gambier Bay*, from which even attacks by the intrepid [destroyers] *Johnston* and *Heermann* did not divert her. The escort carrier, after a salvo-chasing snake dance lasting 25 minutes, began to take 8-inch hits, and dropped astern. The other three heavies, light cruiser *Noshiro*, and a Japanese destroyer now concentrated on *Gambier Bay*. As she began

to sink Captain Vieweg gave the order Abandon Ship. *Chikuma* continued to pound her at short range, and at 0907 she capsized and went down.

On to the southwestward plunged the other five American flattops. *White Plains* fired her single 5-inch guns at each cruiser which closed within 18,000 yards, and made at least six hits on *Chokai*. "Hold on a little longer, boys," sang out Chief Gunner's Mate Jenkins. "We're sucking 'em into 40-mm range!" And they almost did, or would have, but for an attack on that heavy cruiser by four Avengers led by Commander R. L. Fowler of *Kitkun Bay*'s air group. These planes scored ten hits and had the satisfaction of seeing *Chokai* go down. Next, *Chikuma* was sunk by a well coordinated Wildcat-Avenger attack from Felix Stump's Taffy [Task Force] 2; and down she went. Clifton Sprague's harried and beset carriers now threatened by high-caliber battleship fire as well as by *Haguro* and *Tone*, saw to their amazement both heavy cruisers break off their pursuit. A moment later a signalman on the bridge of *Fanshaw Bay* yelled "Goddammit, boys, they're getting away!" The entire [Japanese] Center Force was retiring.

islands leading to Japan began, the kami-kazes were tenacious. More carriers, including the veteran *Saratoga*, were struck. But the constant attacks on Japanese air bases diminished the threat. The Japanese turned to one final weapon as the U.S. invasion of Okinawa was under way. The pride of the Imperial fleet, the battleship *Yamato*, was sent to attack the American fleet. The *Yamato* was a superbattleship, larger and with more firepower than anything in the U.S. Navy. But it was still a battleship, a vessel that had been made strikingly less invincible by the advent of carriers. Twelve U.S. carriers were sent to intercept the *Yamato*. With hundreds of planes sent in to attack, the super-battleship was sunk, along with Japan's hope of winning the war.

The American carriers waited silently off Japan's coast, awaiting the coming invasion of the home islands. The anticipated event, however, never came. On August 6 and August 9, 1945, atomic bombs were dropped on two Japanese cities. These new weapons seemed to have brought Japan to its knees, for the nation surrendered on August 15. Admiral Mitscher, the new head of naval aviation, knew otherwise. In a press release that acknowledged the combined efforts of the American troops in the Pacific, Mitscher attested, "Japan is beaten, and carrier supremacy defeated her."[26]

Chapter 4

The Fighter Plane: Duels in the Sky

Like much of the technology seen in the 1940s, the fighter plane was first developed in World War I. The biplanes and triplanes of that war were made of canvas stretched over wooden frames. Their role was to harass enemy troop movements on the ground, destroy enemy observation balloons, protect bombers, and, of course, shoot down enemy planes. The fighter planes of the Second World War evolved in their construction and performance, but—aside from no longer having to worry about observation balloons—their role remained similar to that of their predecessors. Two functions, however, became predominant, and alterations to design during the war reflected these primary roles. Thus, nearly all of the modifications made to fighters were to enhance their ability either to intercept incoming planes or to accompany and defend bomber planes.

On the heels of World War I, military aeronautics changed rapidly. Although biplanes were still in use throughout the 1940s, the monoplane supplanted them. In most instances the new aircraft were made of metal, not wood, and they incorporated such features as enclosed cockpits and retractable landing gears, both innovations to increase flight speed and give the plane a longer range. The 1930s became the trial period for the modern warplanes. Events in the Pacific and Europe allowed future aggressors to perfect their fighter planes and train their crews.

Air Superiority in the Pacific

In China, Japanese aggressions had turned to war. The inexperienced Japanese pilots were quick to establish air superiority. China had only a few obsolete planes in its air force, none of which was capable of matching the performance and firepower of Japan's Mitsubishi A6M Type O fighter plane. Nicknamed the Zero or Zeke by Allied pilots, the plane was armed with two 7.7-mm machine guns in the fuselage and two 20-mm cannon in the wings. It could fly over

330 mph and had a range of 1,600 miles (over 1,900 miles when carrying an extra drop tank of fuel). The Zero dominated the skies over China despite the fact that it was fragile and poorly armored. Its lack of protective metal plating, however, gave the Zero great maneuverability. The fledgling Chinese air force could not stand up to the Zero's might, so China sought foreign aid.

In 1937, Chinese general Chiang Kai-shek enlisted the help of a retired U.S. Air Corps officer named Claire Lee Chennault. Given command over the fighter defense of China, Chennault returned to the United States to buy planes and hire pilots. America was not at war with Japan, so it could not send its combat pilots to China. Instead, President Franklin Roosevelt, who was sympathetic to China's plight, allowed officers in the military reserve to resign their commissions and join Chennault's volunteer air force. Chennault had the authority to offer these pilots $600 a month to serve plus a $500 bounty for each enemy plane shot down. Because the pay was a lot higher than what they received in the U.S. reserves, there was no shortage of American volunteers. More than a hundred men from all branches of the service enlisted. In 1941, when they reached China and flew under the Chinese flag, the mercenary air force became known as the Flying Tigers.

Flying Tigers to Wildcats

For his pilots, Chennault purchased American Curtiss P-40 Warhawks, the latest American fighter to roll off U.S. assembly lines.

This American fighter has a single wing, an enclosed cockpit, and retractable landing gear. These features set modern warplanes apart from World War I models.

A Chinese soldier guards a squadron of Flying Tigers. The planes are Curtiss P-40 Warhawks.

Because of its heavy, metal construction, the P-40 was slower and less maneuverable than the Zero, but it was also more rugged. In the hands of a skilled pilot, the P-40 could use its weight and its maximum speed of 340 mph to its advantage when diving on enemy planes from above. This meant that the American pilot couldn't engage a Zero in a dogfight, but after making the diving pass, the weight of the P-40 would help him get away without fear of retribution. This tactic proved so effective that the Flying Tigers were credited with 286 Japanese kills while suffering the loss of only 8 pilots themselves. Furthermore, the diving maneuver was

taught to American pilots flying any planes that were slower and heavier than those of their opponents in all stages of the coming war.

Despite the help of the Flying Tigers, the Zero maintained Japanese air superiority in China. When Japan sought to expand its empire in 1941 by seizing most of Southeast Asia and attacking the United States, the Zero was still the predominant fighter in the Pacific. It was capable of land-based as well as carrier operations. Its main opponent in the carrier war that ensued between 1942 and 1943 was the Grumman F4F Wildcat, which—like the P-40—was heavy and sluggish. The Wildcat had armor and self-sealing fuel tanks (to keep fuel from leaking or catching fire if a bullet punctured the tank) that kept it well defended, but because of the weight, its range was only 770 miles. It had six .50-caliber machine guns that made it a threat if it latched onto an enemy plane's tail, but the Zero was so maneuverable that this rarely happened in one-on-one dogfights. Until 1943, American air losses would be great. But the Americans had a huge populace and industrial might on their side; they could replace their aircraft and personnel at unprecedented speed. The Japanese, however, had difficulty finding the resources and pilots to replenish their combat losses as the war dragged on.

Japan's Warrior Code in the Skies

The Japanese Zero was flimsy in comparison with the armored American planes. Because a hit in the unprotected fuel tanks of a Zero could cause the plane to burst into flames, all Japanese pilots were issued parachutes. Many pilots, however, purposefully left them behind as they took off to battle because they refused to bail out if their plane was hit. When ordered to take along the parachutes, most pilots simply used them as seat cushions, still refusing to wear the harnesses into battle. In his autobiography *Samurai!* Japanese ace Saburo Sakai explains the Japanese pilots' reasons for not donning the chute.

> We had little use for these parachutes, for the only purpose they served for us was to hamstring our cockpit movements in a battle. It was difficult to move our arms and legs quickly when encumbered by chute straps. There was another, and equally compelling, reason for not carrying the chutes into combat. The majority of our battles were fought with enemy fighters over their own fields. It was out of the question to bail out over enemy-held territory, for such a move meant a willingness to be captured, and nowhere in the Japanese military code or in the traditional *Bushido* [Samurai code] could one find the distasteful words, "Prisoner of War." *There were no prisoners.* A man who did not return from a flight was dead. No fighter pilot of any courage would ever permit himself to be captured by the enemy. It was completely unthinkable.

The Coming of the Luftwaffe

For Germany, the situation was somewhat analogous to the progress of Japan in the early war years. Adolf Hitler had tested his air force—the Luftwaffe—in the 1936 Spanish Civil War before incorporating it into his plans for European domination. In 1939, when Germany began the Second World War by invading Poland, the Luftwaffe was an important component of the Nazi blitzkrieg. Blitzkrieg tactics required that ground and air forces work in cohesion; planes would bomb and strafe targets, weakening and confusing defenders, who would then be overrun by armored units and infantry. The fighter planes of the Luftwaffe also attacked enemy columns and trains and shot down any Polish planes that were put into the air.

At the outset of World War II, the Polish air force was paltry, and its few fighter aircraft were relics from the 1920s. The Polish pilots were helplessly outclassed by Germans flying Messerschmitt Bf 109E fighter planes. The Me-109, as it was frequently abbreviated, is considered by many to be one of the best all-around fighter planes in the European Theater. It had a maximum speed of 354 mph and an unmatched climbing speed of 3,100 feet per minute. The Me-109 also possessed a fuel-injected engine that kept the plane from stalling as it dove. The Messerschmitt had no competition in the first year of the war; its pilots ruled the sky over Poland literally unchallenged.

In 1940, when Germany invaded France and the Low Countries, the Me-109 met its first competitors. French pilots were as outclassed as the Poles, and Holland, Belgium, and the Netherlands did not possess a viable air force. But the British, who had an expeditionary force fighting on the Continent, did. Although British pilots were inexperienced, they were tenacious, and their fighter planes were well designed. The Hawker Hurricane and the Supermarine Spitfire were the mainstays of the Royal Air Force (RAF), and both had the capability to contend with the Me-109. Yet, on the Continent, the RAF was consistently outperformed, owing largely to the green (inexperienced) crews inside the British cockpits.

The Battle of Britain

When France fell in June 1940, Britain was left standing alone against the German juggernaut. Invasion of the British

A Messerschmitt Me-109 prowls the skies over Poland. The 109 had no challengers until the Luftwaffe encountered the Royal Air Force.

Isles seemed imminent, and the Germans were quick to initiate an air campaign against England to soften up defenses. Heinkel 111 and Dornier 17 bombers clouded the skies over the southern coast of Britain, attacking British airstrips and radar stations, the two military targets that made up Britain's air defense. The radar towers that stretched along the shores were key to the island's protection, for it was only by radar's advance warning of incoming German planes that RAF pilots had enough time to scramble their aircraft and meet the threat. The Germans were excellent bombardiers, however, and the radar stations and nearby airfields were under constant bombardment.

The Germans also sent nine hundred of their Messerschmitt 109 fighters over Britain

Finger Four

Pilots in the Royal Air Force were trained to fly in tight formations of three planes either abreast or in a V shape. This was designed to concentrate firepower, as each plane peeled off and dove at an enemy. Staying in close order and avoiding collision, however, took much of the airman's attention away from scanning the sky for the enemy. The close order was also vulnerable when attacked from above or behind. German fighter pilots, on the other hand, had experimented with an improved, loose formation in the proving grounds of the Spanish Civil War. In his book on the Battle of Britain, author Len Deighton describes this tactically superior formation and how the British were quick to adopt it.

German fighter tactics were based on the *Schwarm*—what Allied pilots called the "finger four"—devised by the great German ace [Werner] Mölders in the Spanish Civil War. A is the leader, B is the wingman who never leaves his side. He flies on the sun side of the leader and low so that the others do not have to look into the glare of the sun to see him.

C is the leader of the second *Rotte* [pair]; D is his wingman. In each pair, one man is leader and attacker while the wingman is de-

fender. The two-man unit proved far more psychologically and tactically effective than the traditional three employed by the RAF, who soon adopted the pair system. Fighter Command also learnt from the Luftwaffe to fly in open formations, more difficult to spot in an empty sky than a tight squadron line abreast.

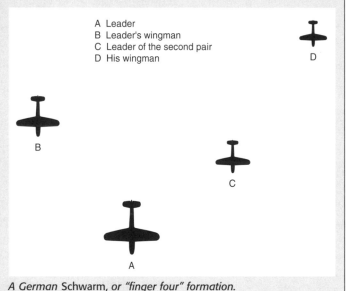

A Leader
B Leader's wingman
C Leader of the second pair
D His wingman

A German Schwarm, *or "finger four" formation.*

to protect some eleven hundred bombers. The Me-109's biggest disadvantage, however, was its limited range. Although it could accompany bombers to their targets in southern England, its low fuel capacity didn't allow it to engage British interceptors for extended periods of time. Thus, even though the British planes might have been inferior to the Me-109 in some respects, they literally had the time to fly circles around the Germans.

The primary British interceptors were the Hurricane and the Spitfire, the same aircraft that had fought in France. The older

Hawker Hurricane was the most numerous of the British defenders. It was 30 mph slower than the Me-109, but it was heavily armored and fitted with a deadly complement of eight machine guns. The Me-109 was a much more agile plane, and Luftwaffe ace Adolf Galland simply wrote the Hurricane off as "hopeless—a nice airplane to shoot down."[27] Yet the Hurricane was still responsible for 75 percent of the kills in the Battle of Britain. Of course, most of these kills were German bombers, not fighters. The Supermarine Spitfire was the British plane that bore the responsibility of engaging the Me-109.

With a ceiling of forty-two thousand feet (two thousand feet higher than the Hurricane), the Spitfire could chase the Me-109s, which typically flew escort above the bombers in their charge. The Spitfire was nearly as modern an aircraft as the Messerschmitt. It had a top speed of 370 mph, and it could outturn, if not outclimb, the Me-109. Like the Hurricane, it was fitted with eight machine guns in its wings. Whereas he

Three British Spitfires scramble to intercept approaching German planes. The Spitfire was comparable to the Me-109 in performance.

had condemned the Hurricane, Adolf Galland admitted, "The Spitfire was dangerous, on account of its armament, climb, manoeuvrability, and the courage of its pilots."[28] But the Spitfires existed in limited quantities, and experienced pilots were even more of a commodity.

Although fearsome counterparts to the Me-109s, the Spitfires and their pilots were constantly taxed. British airmen were almost continuously in the air or on alert as successive waves of German planes crossed the English Channel. As British military aviation expert Norman Franks describes, "Readiness states varied from cockpit 'standby' of two minutes or readiness in the dispersal hut (or outside it in the sunshine) of five minutes. From time to time the squadron might be put down at 15 or 30 minutes availability, which gave the pilots time to go for a wash or bath or a hot meal."[29] While the professional men were exhausted, the replacement pilots were usually poorly trained. These new pilots were taken from all branches of the military, given slight training, and rushed into combat, sometimes within hours. Though some replacements were quick to adapt and become veterans, many were easy prey for the experienced German airmen. All in all, Britain's air defenses were crumbling. Even at the outset of the fight, the nation had only between six hundred and seven hundred aircraft to defend all of

Britain, not just the southern coast. Many of these planes were perishing in the skies and on the ground. The constant pummeling of British air bases and the large numbers of British planes shot down took their toll on the nation's war effort.

The Blitz

The reprieve came in August 1940. Throughout recent German bombardments, a few stray planes had accidentally dropped their payloads on suburbs of London instead of on military targets. In retaliation, British prime minister Winston Churchill ordered British bombers to intentionally attack Berlin. On the night of August 25, British planes bombed the German capital. The raid caused little damage, but it sent Hitler into a rage. He had already erro-

London burns during the blitz. Hitler's switch to civilian targets allowed the British to rebuild their airfields and replace lost aircraft.

neously concluded that, because of continued German aircraft losses, the attacks on British airfields were ineffective. Coupled with the audacity of the raid on Berlin, Hitler felt that a new strategy was needed. He gave his Luftwaffe commander, Hermann Göring, free rein to implement a plan of reprisal, ordering German bombers to strike London in a vain effort to bring the British government to its knees. On September 7, the first assault—carried out by three hundred bombers and six hundred escorting fighters—caught Britain off guard. The RAF was prepared to defend its airfields, not its capital. Few interceptors reached the incoming bombers, but several squadrons were airborne when the German planes were retreating toward the coast. They took many of the bombers out of the sky but also lost many pilots to the German escorts. The air battle cost both sides dearly, and the population of London had had its first taste of the coming blitz.

Hitler's switching from military to civilian targets gave England the time it needed to recuperate. Although the people of London suffered almost nightly, British airfields were rebuilt and more planes were manufactured and rushed to the battlefront. In addition, since London was farther inland than previous targets, the German planes spent so much of their fuel reaching the city that the fighter escorts had little time to engage the British planes before having to turn back home. The British pilots had time on their side. They also had the opportunity to harry the incoming bombers and escorts

all the way to London and all along the return route. On September 15, one of the largest German sorties made the trek to London. The massive bombardment was meant to be a prelude to an amphibious invasion. British pilots had been given advanced warning by radar, and squadrons were in the air all along the path of attack. As Norman Franks writes,

> The tenacity of the RAF fighter pilots as well as the sheer number of fighters they could see, must have come as a great shock to many Luftwaffe flyers. It had been confidently predicted that [Britain's] Fighter Command was down to its last "handful" of aircraft, and yet the Luftwaffe could see flight after flight, squadron after squadron, heading straight for them, their wing guns blazing.[30]

The constant sniping by the British claimed sixty German aircraft. The RAF had lost twenty-six. Though the attackers reached London and dropped their bombs, the mission had been disastrous. The loss of so many aircraft and the discovery that the RAF was still a threat convinced Hitler that his plans for invading England should be scrapped.

From September 15 on, the tide had turned in Britain's favor. The remaining bombing missions sent over England suffered increasing losses. By October 1940, the war in the skies over England had effectively been won. The growing number of

Spitfires and Hurricanes made daylight raids too costly for the Germans, thus they were forced to run them at night when the fear of interception was lessened, but so was the accuracy of bombing. The Battle of Britain was over. The Germans had lost 1,733 aircraft; the British had lost 915. The Luftwaffe was badly decimated. Hermann Göring pulled most of the remaining planes from the British front and put them on standby for their next great invasion—Operation Barbarossa, the assault on Russia.

Evolution

The Battle of Britain was England's finest hour in World War II. The German Messerschmitt had proved vulnerable to RAF fighters and pilots. Germany's response was commonplace; it needed to produce an even better fighter plane. So while the Supermarine Spitfire was being continually upgraded, the Germans turned to a new design. They developed the Focke-Wulf 190. The Focke-Wulf was a superb aircraft with a top speed of about 450 mph. Typical variants of the plane carried two machine guns in the nose and four 20-mm cannon in the wings. In 1940, when the first Fw-190s came off the assembly line, an impressed Hermann Göring exclaimed, "We must turn these new fighters out like so many hot rolls!"[31] Yet the Germans still had faith in the Messerschmitt, and despite the Focke-Wulf's evident superiority, the Me-109 continued to be manufactured in greater numbers.

The Focke-Wulf's supremacy lasted until the United States entered the war in Eu-

rope. The Americans had suffered with sluggish aircraft in the Pacific Theater until the arrival of the Grumman F6F-5 Hellcat in 1943, and then the fortunes of America's aeronautical engineering were assured. The Hellcat was able to outperform the mighty Japanese Zero and, together with the more powerful Chance Vought F4U Corsair, was able to achieve mastery over the Japanese fighters in the Pacific. When the Americans turned their attention to defeating Germany, they developed fighters that could compete with and eventually outperform the Luftwaffe.

The Republic P-47 Thunderbolt was one of the most versatile U.S. planes to see action in Europe. It could reach a top speed of 429 mph and had a ceiling of 40,000 feet. The P-47 was a large, awkward-looking plane on the ground, but in the air it had the firepower and maneuverability to take on the Focke-Wulf and later versions of the Me-109. Its most memorable role, however, was not in engaging enemy fighters but in shooting up enemy ground targets. Carrying two 1,000-pound bombs and up to ten 5-inch rockets, the ground-attack versions of the Thunderbolt ripped apart German airfields and railroads. In over 500,000 sorties, the Thunderbolt was responsible for the destruction of 9,000 locomotives and 160,000 railroad cars, as well as the shooting down of nearly 12,000 enemy planes.

The Mustang

The Thunderbolt was a powerful aircraft; in fact, most American aces of the war

(Top to bottom) A Chance Vought F4U Corsair, three Republic P-47 Thunderbolts, four North American P-51 Mustangs.

North American P-51 Mustang. The Mustang was a truly unique airplane. While most fighter aircraft could not travel long distances, the Mustang had a range of eight hundred miles without spare fuel tanks. With extra tanks, it could accompany Allied bombers to and from their targets in Germany, thus neutralizing the Luftwaffe's advantage over the unescorted sorties that had made the runs prior to 1944. The Allied bomber crews were thankful for the new protection. One bomber crewman was especially appreciative of the P-51 that fended off the Luftwaffe from attacking his plane. "The name of that fighter plane was 'Linda,'" he remarked, "and it's no coincidence that my first daughter's name is Linda. I feel that I never would have been there had it not been for that P-51."[32]

Originally the Mustang was developed for British use. The English were impressed but felt that the American engine was underpowered. The RAF's opinion was that the P-51 was "a bloody good airplane, only it needs a bit more poke."[33] The British replaced the American engine with one from a Spitfire. The result was surprising. Fuel efficiency was paramount, and yet the plane could still reach 440 mph. The United States quickly ordered twenty-two hundred of the Spitfire's Rolls Royce Merlin engines for their own Mustangs.

achieved their records flying the P-47. Yet it would not be the plane most remembered by WWII pilots. That honor went to the

In action, the Mustang was first restricted to accompanying bombers, flying tightly with the bomber formations. Although they could protect their charges, the Mustangs were not permitted to break formation and pursue the enemy planes. When General James Doolittle took command of the 8th Air Force in 1944, he cancelled that rule. Doolittle emphasized that the role of the Mustang should be to aggressively knock enemy planes from the air to clear the skies and pave the way for upcoming invasions into Europe. No longer chained to the bombers, the Mustangs became the terror of the skies. In combat, the P-51 squadrons were claiming seven enemy aircraft for every one Mustang lost. During March and April 1944, one fighter group of Mustangs destroyed a remarkable 235 German planes in the sky and another 125 on the ground.

The Advent of Jets

Germany was continually upgrading its planes throughout the declining years of the war, but no conventional design seemed capable of dealing with the Mustang. Furthermore, thanks to Allied bombing and strafing, the Luftwaffe's numbers were dropping. Even if the later Focke-Wulfs could compete with the Mustangs, Germany could never put more than a squadron of them in the air. But Germany was making technological headway. In 1942, Germany had already begun experimenting with jet propulsion. The Messerschmitt factory had devised a

fighter plane in that year that relied on the new technology. Dubbed the *Schwalbe* (Swallow), the Me-262A, powered by two Junkers Jumo gas turbine engines, was faster than anything the Allies could muster. The German high command, however, believed the new high-speed aircraft was not needed; the propeller-driven Me-109 and Fw-190 were already achieving great success. When the Allies began to gain in the battle for air superiority, production of Me-262s resumed. As the first jet fighters came out of the factories in 1943, they encountered further obstacles. Primarily, Hitler felt that the jets should be used as bombers, not fighters. On his order, the Me-262 was redesigned to function as a bomber, but the conversion reduced the plane's flight speed. At 420 mph, the jet could still be matched by the Allied propeller planes. In fact, a Spitfire was the first plane to shoot down an Me-262. Airman Heinz Knoke was one of many who saw the potential of the Me-262 being sacrificed to Hitler's whim. At the time, Knoke wrote,

> Following an idiotic order given by Hitler a few weeks ago, the first jets to come off the assembly line are to be used only for purposes of "reprisal.". . . If we could only have one or two Wings [groups] operating with the new Me-262s, there would still be a good chance for the German Fighter Command to save the situation. Otherwise the war in the air will be lost.[34]

The Mustang and the Swallow

In his book *Mustang at War,* Roger A. Freeman notes how the P-51 fared against the new German jet plane, the Me-262. Recognizing the strengths of the jet fighter, Mustang pilots had to rely on everything from uncontrollable luck to clever tactics to successfully counter the new threat.

The Me 262 began to appear in a fighter role during October 1944 and though undoubtedly scored many successes, Allied fighters were able to bring down a number of the jets. In early incidents German pilots were caught off guard or mechanical difficulties gave the Allied pilots an advantage.

Mustangs, foremost in these encounters, eventually improved interception techniques to bring a steady flow of victories. Many were obtained by loitering in the area of known Me 262 bases and waiting until the jets were in the vulnerable position of taking-off or landing. The speed gap between the Me 262 and the Mustang under combat conditions was not all that great and an unwary Me 262 pilot, cruising at 400 to 450 mph was not a difficult quarry if the P-51 pilot had an altitude advantage.

A Messerschmitt Me-262A Schwalbe, or "Swallow."

The conversion also caused delays in getting the plane into squadrons. Furthermore, late in 1944, Hitler changed his mind and had the Me-262 converted back to a fighter. By the time the new Me-262 saw action, it proved its power (an astonishing speed of 540 mph), but it had come too late to affect the outcome of the war. Only one hundred had gotten into service by war's end. Knoke was correct: The air war had been lost.

The advent of the jet age foretold how future air wars would be fought. Jet propulsion would be harnessed for wars in Korea and, later, Vietnam. Propeller planes did not disappear, however. In fact, the Mustang continued its role as a fighter throughout the Korean War. The experiments of a defeated Germany, however, presaged the future of aviation. Many contemporary historians continue to debate whether larger quantities of the jet fighters manufactured at Germany's earliest possible convenience could have, indeed, changed the outcome of the air war in Europe.

Chapter 5

The Bomber: The Air War over Germany

Bomber aircraft in the Second World War came in two varieties. Tactical bombers such as the fearsome German Junkers Ju-87 Stuka were designed to fly close support for ground troops. At low altitudes, these planes would drop their one or two bombs—with relative precision—on enemy tanks, infantry, or defensive positions. Strategic bombers were quite different. These were the larger planes that flew at high altitudes and dropped entire racks of bombs on targets behind enemy lines. The targets of the strategic bombers were industrial facilities, ports, or military installations, and the tons of bombs that fell from entire squadrons of these aircraft usually destroyed their targets by saturating the area with explosions. The great disadvantage to strategic bombing was—and still is—the nearly inevitable loss of civilian life, since most of the strategic targets were located in major cities.

The idea of strategic bombing came in the interim years between the two world wars. Military aviation leaders foresaw the

possibility of crippling an enemy nation's war effort by sending bomb-laden aircraft to industrial targets deep in enemy territory and then destroying them, effectively reducing the opponent's ability to manufacture materials needed to continue making war. Colonel J. F. C. Fuller of the British Air Command predicted in 1920 that, in the next war, "Fleets of aeroplanes will attack the enemy's great industrial and governing centres. All these attacks will be made against the civil population in order to compel it to accept the will of the attacker."[35] Fuller and his compatriots Captain Basil Liddell Hart and Sir Hugh Trenchard, along with Italian general Giulio Douhet and American general William Mitchell, could see the coming age of warfare. Each pressed his respective nation to consider the strategic implications of bombing enemy infrastructure, and all encouraged their governments to develop the planes to accomplish such raids.

Sir Hugh Trenchard was the main proponent of creating a strategic bombing ca-

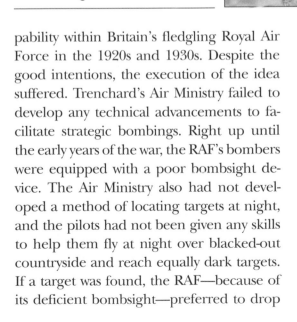

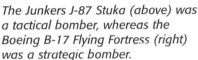
The Junkers J-87 Stuka (above) was a tactical bomber, whereas the Boeing B-17 Flying Fortress (right) was a strategic bomber.

pability within Britain's fledgling Royal Air Force in the 1920s and 1930s. Despite the good intentions, the execution of the idea suffered. Trenchard's Air Ministry failed to develop any technical advancements to facilitate strategic bombings. Right up until the early years of the war, the RAF's bombers were equipped with a poor bombsight device. The Air Ministry also had not developed a method of locating targets at night, and the pilots had not been given any skills to help them fly at night over blacked-out countryside and reach equally dark targets. If a target was found, the RAF—because of its deficient bombsight—preferred to drop

many bombs of less destructive power over the area, hoping to score at least one hit, rather than drop one large bomb capable of fully eliminating a target. The largest impediment to an effective bombing strategy, however, was the British Air Ministry's reluctance to bomb targets near civilian centers. The British did not want to be labeled ruthless murderers of innocents, and they feared that if they blatantly killed noncombatants, the enemy might respond in kind and bomb England's cities. All of these obstacles greatly hindered the RAF's strategic bombing program. In 1939 when Hugh Trenchard retired from the Air Ministry,

England had the enthusiasm for using its bombers but it lacked the technology and decisiveness to carry out an effective campaign.

Britain's Early Campaign

When World War II erupted and the British were in the thick of the fight to defend France, Belgium, the Netherlands, and Luxembourg, the RAF remained hampered for some time. Instead of bombing Germany's industrial centers, the British bombers were used ineffectively against frontline targets. It was the more advanced Nazi tactics that convinced Britain to rethink its strategy. In May 1940, the German Luftwaffe bombed the Dutch port of Rotterdam. Although the raid killed only one thousand civilians, the media inflated the number to as high as thirty thousand. Because of the heinous act, Britain removed some of the moral objections it had to bombing German cities. That month the RAF was given permission to start bombing military installations on the eastern bank of the Rhine.

Germany continued to utilize its strategic bombing capabilities to great effect throughout the war. French cities, Norwegian ports, Greek hill towns, and Russian industrial centers all suffered under the bombs of the Luftwaffe at different stages of the war. England during the 1940s was perhaps the most notable target of the German air force. The con-tinuous attacks on British air bases, manufacturing works, and eventually the population of London nearly destroyed the British war effort. However, the Allies conducted the most protracted and strategically decisive bombing campaign in the entire war. The British attacks on German railway centers and oil refineries in May 1940, were just the first stages of a much larger scheme that would eventually bring Germany to military and economic ruin.

Initial British raids into Germany were few and far between. England did not have enough bombers to make continual forays into Germany. It also didn't have enough fighter planes (most were busy defending England from Germany's bombing campaign) to protect the bombers it could send. Thus, the numbers of bomber aircraft avail-

After the Luftwaffe bombed Rotterdam (pictured), the British overcame their reluctance to strike at civilian targets in Germany.

able were further decimated by the expertly trained Luftwaffe fighters that defended the skies over Germany. The main British bomber also proved inefficient in its role. The Blenheim was poorly defended and 200 mph slower than the German fighters that pursued it. The aircraft carried only a 1,000-pound bomb payload, which, scattered among five to ten bombs, was quite negligible. In August 1941, after nearly half of a squadron of Blenheims was shot down attacking shipping and port facilities in the now German-occupied Rotterdam, British prime minister Winston Churchill sent encouraging words to the crews:

> The devotion of the attacks on Rotterdam and other objectives are beyond all praise. The Charge of the Light Brigade at Balaclava is eclipsed in brightness by these almost daily deeds of fame.[36]

The Charge of the Light Brigade was a wasteful and tragic—though nonetheless brave—cavalry charge made during the Crimean War. Although the comparison to the heroic charge was meant to be praiseworthy, the inherent sense of futile sacrifice could not have been more profound. The lackluster Blenheim and its associates, the Hampden, Battle, and Whitley, were insufficient for the job. Flying at night to stay concealed, the planes' poor direction-finding capabilities and their obsolete bombsight (especially at night) made each raid nearly inconsequential.

As the war progressed, Britain's choice of targets changed. Oil refineries and railroad yards were its first common targets. The theory was that oil was the chief ingredient of the mechanized warfare of the blitzkrieg. However, the ineffectual night raids were proving to have little effect on Germany's manufacturing and transport of fuel. In fact, in August 1941, bomber command received reports that only a tiny fraction of its bombers were hitting within miles of their designated targets. With the rise of German submarine warfare and the growing losses at sea, bomber command decided to concentrate more on known port facilities in occupied France that harbored the deadly U-boats. Attacks on these submarine pens were equally ineffectual, primarily because the U-boats were serviced in large concrete sheds built into the protective earthen shoreline. Still, throughout all such missions, the goal had been to avoid mass civilian casualties. As the war progressed, however, and London suffered under bombings aimed directly at the populace, Churchill asked for retaliation. Until then, the German citizenry had escaped the horrors of war while the Dutch, the Belgians, the French, and now the British had been made targets. Churchill recognized that the decision would not be embraced by many members of the British Parliament. He was nonetheless resolute. In a letter to a minister in aircraft production, Churchill noted,

> We have no Continental Army which can defeat the German military power.

The [naval] blockade is broken and Hitler has Asia and probably Africa to draw from. Should he be repulsed here or not try invasion, he will recoil eastward, and we have nothing to stop him. But there is one thing that will bring

Rituals of Survival

In his book *Bomber Command,* historian Max Hastings acknowledges that every bombing run was filled with risk and that the crew's survival was subject to blind chance. But by being rigorous on the ground and attentive in the air, airmen could increase the odds that their fate would not be determined by their lack of preparation. In the following anecdote, Hastings describes the rituals of one Canadian bomber pilot who survived several missions over Germany.

A pilot such as Micky Martin was daring in the air, but also very careful. He and his crew checked every detail of their own aircraft before take-off, far more meticulously than routine demanded. Martin personally polished every inch of Perspex on his cockpit canopy. At 10,000 feet over Germany at night, a fighter was no more than a smear at the corner of a man's eye until it fired. Martin studied the techniques for improving his own vision, moving his head backwards and forwards constantly, to distinguish between the reality and the optical illusion beyond the windscreen. He taxied the aircraft to the butts before each trip so that his gunners could realign their Brownings [machine guns]. Every man who survived Bomber Command agrees that luck was critical: however brilliant a flier, he was vulnerable to the Russian roulette of a predicted flak barrage. But a careful crew could increase their chance of survival a hundred per cent.

him back and bring him down, and that is an absolutely devastating, exterminating attack by very heavy bombers from this country upon the Nazi homeland.[37]

By 1942, German cities still remained untouched, but their fate had been decided. Bomber command had been given the go-ahead in 1941 but was unable to coordinate reprisal raids yet given the continuing need to strike at military targets. The plans, however, had been laid, and a new string of heavy bombers came into being in anticipation of the forthcoming missions.

New Bombers and New Technology

The Short Stirling and the Handley-Page Halifax were sturdier aircraft than the mid-level Blenheim, and they carried 5-ton bomb loads. The drawback was the lengthy amount of time required to build the heavy bombers. Roughly five Spitfire fighters could be manufactured in the same amount of time required to make one Halifax, and the Spitfires were needed to stave off the German bombers. In November 1941, the Air Ministry decided to scale back its missions over Germany in the hopes of building up a stronger air fleet that could stage large-scale bombing runs in the future. The buildup never materialized, however, because planes were constantly needed to counter German warships and submarines in the Atlantic. Yet better bombers did appear. Besides the Halifax and Stirling, the most impressive of the new heavy bombers was the Avro Lancaster. The Lancaster was a four-engine aircraft that could cruise at nearly 220 mph and rise to twenty thousand feet. It had a payload that increased over the years from four thousand pounds to twenty-two thousand pounds. While the Halifax and Stirling would be phased out by 1944, the Lancaster would remain the primary British bomber until the end of the war.

Along with new planes, the British had also developed a new navigation tool that used radio signals received from England to fix a plane's position. For the first time, RAF bombers could find their way over Germany in the dark and in inclement weather with relative accuracy. Thus the year 1942 proved to be the advent of a greatly improved bombing campaign. Although certainly improved, the effort still paled in comparison to coming years. With the RAF still trying to

gather its strength, the number of missions sent into Germany was quite low. Only 6,485 tons of bombs fell on German cities in June 1942; 57,267 tons would fall in the same month only two years later. Still, massive raids did hit Cologne, Essen, and Bremen in Germany's industrial Ruhr Valley. And the Lancasters were proving their capability. Delivering the heaviest payloads, these planes were usually sent in the second wave to bomb a target because they were considered tough enough to withstand the antiaircraft barrages from the fully awakened defenders. Britain had found its bomber and its navigational device. Now it just needed time to manufacture more planes.

The impressive Avro Lancaster served as the primary British bomber in the later stages of World War II.

America Enters the War

By the end of 1942, the British had only 515 frontline bombers (178 of which were Lancasters). In that year, however, the bombing campaign got an overdue shot in the arm. The United States had joined the war in 1941, but most of its military force was tied up in the Pacific fighting Japan. It had lent Britain armaments, including airplanes, but with the invasion of North Africa and then Italy in 1943, the United States finally brought its full military participation to the European Theater. The U.S. 8th Air Force was stationed in Britain, and the Lancaster was now supported by the mighty B-17 Flying Fortress. The B-17 was an enormous four-engine aircraft. It could climb to 33,000 feet and travel at 260 mph. Though the later variants had a payload of 17,600 pounds, the Flying Fortresses still carried fewer bombs than the British Lancasters. But they bristled with defensive machine guns: thirteen in total, including hydraulically operated turrets on the top, bottom, and chin of the aircraft. More important than the plane, however, was its unique Norden bombsight, a mechanical calculator that computed trajectory. The Norden gave the Americans more accurate bombing capability, unlike the British, who were still relying on rather wasteful area bombing.

The debate over the advantages and disadvantages of area bombing was only one issue that separated the British and American bombing strategies. The Americans pre-

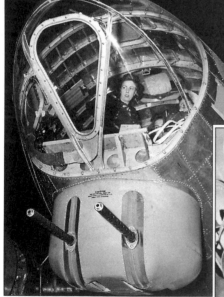

The B-17 featured a chin turrett (seen above at one of Boeing's factories) and the extremely accurate Norden bombsight (right).

ferred daylight raids to increase the chances of hitting the correct target, while the British still preferred the protective cover of darkness. The Americans also believed that their well-armed Flying Fortresses were quite capable of reaching their targets unescorted. "We tried to warn them against this," RAF marshal Sholto Douglas wrote, "basing our warning on our own bitter experiences. But the Americans were so sure about their own theories, and they would not listen to us, which was sad because we had learned our lessons in a very hard school."[38] Yet the B-17 proved itself a powerful weapon that, when flown in formation with other B-17s so that the multiple machine guns provided overlapping fields of fire, could manage quite successfully to reach targets without fighter protection.

The British remained unconvinced, and on the first few missions, the B-17s were given lightly defended targets in France, Holland, and Belgium—places that fighter escorts could reach. Although meant to be a training ground for the inexperienced American crews, these missions also proved to be the testing ground for the Norden bombsight, which was living up to the claim that it could "drop a bomb in a pickle barrel." The effect on the morale of American crews, though, was not to be ignored. B-17 pilot Walter Kelly boasted—if prematurely—"We now provided ample evidence

B-17s fly in a "combat box" formation as one of the planes releases its bombs.

of who was to be boss of daytime air over western Europe."[39]

Even if some pilots assumed themselves to be the "boss of daytime air," others were more realistic. Pilot John Regan attested, "Fortunately for me at the time, the Germans didn't know how to attack the B-17, which was still an airplane with which they were not familiar."[40] The missions into France were also protected by P-47 Thunderbolts. Once the B-17 ventured unescorted into Germany and the Luftwaffe negotiated the plane's weak spots, the Flying Fortress could be knocked down like any other bomber. To improve their survivability, however, the Allies came up with "combat box" formation, in which six to nine B-17s would fly in a rectangular pattern while an equal number of B-17s flew in the

The Ball Turret

One of the defensive features of the B-17 Flying Fortress was a hydraulically operated turret attached to the belly of the aircraft. Called the ball turret, it was a confined space that housed one gunner and a pair of machine guns. Throughout the bomber's journey, the ball gunner would remain hunched inside the Perspex glass cupola facing the earth below, seeming to hang in space. In his book on the B-17, Roger A. Freeman writes about this unique feature of the plane and the men who occupied it.

Ask any man who went to war in a Fortress which was the worst crew position on the aircraft and the chances are he will immediately reply, "The ball turret". Indeed, this tight little glazed sphere buttoned to the underside of the fuselage needed a stout-hearted occupant, immune from claustrophobia and bolstered against the thought of being without a parachute if the aircraft was suddenly stricken. So cramped was the gunner's position that an early British assessment of the turret considered it quite untenable for long flights—there were many American airmen who would have agreed. If one had no qualms about the angle at which the world below was viewed, the ball provided an extraordinary vantage point. Ironically, far from being the most dangerous place in a B-17 as the majority thought, statistical evidence later proved it to be the safest—at least so far as battle wounds were concerned. This is explained by the huddled posture of the gunner, back against the armour plated door. Towards the end of the war in Europe, when fighter attacks became rare, there was a plan to remove all ball turrets from B-17s to save weight—substantial at 1200 lbs plus the gunner—and add speed through reduced drag, but this was never instituted.

Members of a ground crew examine the ball turret of a B-17.

same pattern a thousand feet higher up and staggered from the first group. Any German fighter plane that entered that "box" between the two formations was sure to be hit by the intense, overlapped fire from all the bombers. Similarly, the sides of the "box" were protected because planes to the side and above (or below) could help fend off fighters from a B-17 that was under attack. The new formation also allowed the B-17s to drop their bombs in a much tighter pattern, helping saturate a target with explosions. Yet even with the improved tactics, the experienced Luftwaffe pilots could still decimate the bomber groups, and the accuracy of German antiaircraft fire was not affected by formation flying.

While the Americans trained, the British had been carrying on their attacks on the Ruhr for four and a half months. Sarcastically nicknamed the "Happy Valley" by bomber crews who were pummeled by fighters and well-organized antiaircraft defenses, the Ruhr Valley was the location of the Krupp arms works, one of the main manufacturers of Germany's weapons, as well as other military supply facilities. In July 1943, the city of Hamburg was bombed repeatedly by waves of seven hundred to eight hundred aircraft. On the second raid, the city was swept by a firestorm from the resulting explosions. Thousands of German civilians suffocated as the flames depleted the oxygen. Estimates of civilian casualties ran as high as forty-two thousand, more people than had been killed in the Luftwaffe's blitz on England. Despite the success at Hamburg, the Ruhr's defenders were tenacious. Bomber command lost nearly one thousand planes in over 18,500 missions flown.

Paying a High Price for Success

In late 1943, the 8th Air Force began its first missions into Germany. In August, 146 B-17s were directed at aircraft factories in Regensburg and ball-bearing plants in Schweinfurt. It was the deepest the Americans had flown into Germany.

Once out of fighter protection, the B-17s were jumped by the Luftwaffe. The Germans had learned to tackle the B-17s from the front because these early Flying Fortresses didn't yet have the rotating nose turret, so the defensive machine guns in front had a limited field of fire. Although coming in head-on required quick reflexes at 500 mph, the Luftwaffe pilots scored many victories with this tactic. Yet the first wave of bombers got off easy. The second wave of 230 B-17s was met by 300 German fighters and well-prepared antiaircraft batteries. A total of 60 bombers were shot down that day, and 17 were damaged beyond repair. It was the 8th Air Force's worst loss to date. A second raid on Schweinfurt was equally disastrous. The 8th Air Force believed the losses to be so

A German gun battery is prepared for action. Formation flying could not protect American bombers from antiaircraft fire.

bad that unescorted bombing runs were temporarily suspended. "Though no formation of American bombers was ever turned back," historian Arthur Gordon writes, "the worst that the opponents of daylight bombing had prophesied had come true. Heavily-armed bombers, it was now seen, could not protect themselves against massive fighter attack."[41]

German industry was being slowed by the round-the-clock bombing (the Americans bombing during the day and the British still bombing at night), but the overall effects were not that telling. The industries were not collapsing. As economist John Kenneth Galbraith described,

> The reasons were threefold. First, the machine tools were relatively invulnerable. They'd be buried under rubble but could be dug out in a day or two. Second, it was possible to decentralize production: to move the machinery into schools and churches. It was reorganized in much less time than was imagined. The Germans discovered it wasn't necessary for production to be in a single factory. They also discovered a large range of substitutes. It was possible to redesign a lot of equipment to reduce the use of ball bearings [for example]. Third, it was possible to reorganize what had been sporadic and less than diligent managements.[42]

The British didn't feel that the ball-bearing plants in Schweinfurt were even worth the effort and sacrifice. They preferred to attack submarine construction facilities and to target industries or repair facilities that seemed to be the assembly points of Germany's weapons. All in all, the campaign had yet to turn the tide of war. Hitler's chief architect, Albert Speer, was an astute observer of the Allied progress in the air. According to historian Max Hastings, Speer "marvelled at the American failure to repeat the two Schweinfurt attacks, at whatever cost. He was amazed that the British, having achieved remarkable success at Hamburg, neither returned to that city in sufficient force to prevent its recovery nor attempted to inflict the same treatment on any other city save Berlin, where the odds were impossible."[43]

In late 1943 through early 1944, British bomber command launched more than nine thousand sorties against the German capital. The trek was difficult because the weather over the north of Germany was cloudy and promised snow or rain through the winter months. Air defenses were strong, and Germany's Luftwaffe still ruled the skies. By January 1944, the British were losing 6 percent of the aircraft sent on the missions. Over the entire campaign against Berlin, the British lost more than a thousand bombers, and another sixteen hundred were damaged. The war ministries claimed success, saying that huge sections of the city had been leveled. The truth, however, was that, despite the losses of buildings and civilians, Berlin's industries were still producing efficiently.

A bomber passes over Berlin. In attacks against the city, the British lost more than a thousand of their planes.

The Americans were not faring any better. By late 1943, they had lost 148 aircraft in four operations. Their tactics in 1944 therefore were changed. They had received two new planes in 1943: the Consolidated Liberator B-24 bomber and the P-51 Mustang fighter. The former was an excellent long-range bomber with a 2,000-mile range and an 8,000-pound bomb load, but the latter was the weapon that changed the fortunes of the 8th Air Force. The P-51 had enough range to accompany bombing raids to and from Germany. In addition, the Mustang was a better fighter plane than those possessed by the Luftwaffe; it knocked most of the German defenders from the sky. Realizing that owning the skies above Germany would greatly assist the bombing campaign, the Americans were bent on a strategy of destroying the Luftwaffe. In the air, the bombers would draw out the German aircraft and then the Mustangs would engage and eliminate them. On the ground, the German air bases and aircraft factories were primary targets of the Liberators and Flying Fortresses. The strategy was successful. German pilots were becoming more and more scarce. Even as its aircraft plants were taking punishment, the Luftwaffe in late 1944 was able to field more planes than qualified pilots.

The End of a Long Campaign

In June 1944, the Allied ground forces landed along the Normandy coast in France. Within a few months of bitter fighting, the Allied armies controlled most of northern France up to the German border on the east. It was a triumph for the foot

Carrying 8,000-pound bomb loads, Consolidated B-24 Liberators head for Germany. Airbases and aircraft factories were their primary targets.

soldiers, but it was a blessing for the bomber crews. Fighter and antiaircraft defenses along former flight paths through France were now gone. The Germans were losing the ground war in the West, and, because the Luftwaffe had been reduced on the eastern front to try to hold back American and British bombers, the Russians were driving beyond their own borders and pushing the Germans back into Poland. At the same time, however, Germany was beginning to use new jet-propelled fighter planes to counter the Allied bombing. The Messerschmitt 262 jet could scream past a B-17 firing its guns, never to be touched by the machine gunners on the Flying Fortress. It was a unique and powerful new weapon that could have potentially disrupted the bombing campaign. But it was not to be. As

Arthur Gordon explains, "Despite these spectacular developments, the whole German war machine by early 1945 was slowly and inexorably grinding to a halt."[44] The jets were not produced in sufficient numbers to make a dramatic impact on the bombing. The Russians had reached the border of Germany in early 1945, and the other Allies had pushed into the Ruhr by April. Once the main target of the campaign, the Ruhr and its factories were in Allied hands. In that month, with no targets left to destroy, the Allies announced the end of the strategic bombing campaign.

★ **Chapter 6** ★

D Day: Everything Put to the Test

Operation Overlord was significant, in part, because it was the first large-scale Allied assault conducted with a truly multinational force. The invasion incorporated troops from the United States, Britain, Canada, France, and Poland. Along with the diverse nationalities, the invasion involved the use of equally varied weaponry. All factions of the military—the army, navy, and air force—staged combined operations to overcome the awesome German defenses. The success of the attack depended on naval gunfire, strategic bombings, paratroop drops, armor and artillery firepower, and the courage of the foot soldier. Only by the combined strengths of these various military assets were the Allied armies able to establish themselves in northern Europe and hasten the drive to the heart of the German empire.

The German defenders were prepared to repel such an invasion. In fact, since the Allies had put men ashore in Italy to the south, the German high command was expecting that—with the short distance between England and the French northern coast—a similar, larger assault would come across the English Channel. In

The German defenses in Normandy included minefields, cement bunkers, and massive German pillboxes such as this one.

anticipation, the Germans had built elaborate defenses and marshaled forces to repulse an attack. The problem the Germans faced was determining where the Allies would most likely come ashore. France had a lengthy coastline, and it would have been unwise for the Germans to disperse their troops along the entire front. Instead, Germany chose to erect the Atlantic Wall, a series of cement bunkers and pillboxes arrayed above the most accessible beaches, with antitank obstacles and minefields dispersed along the water's edge to block easy access to the shore. Into these positions, the Germans could place fewer, less proficient soldiers who needed only to hold back an invasion force until the main body of crack troops and tanks could be moved in from a distant staging point. But where to place these elite forces—along the Normandy coast with its vast beaches or near the Pas de Calais, the beachhead that was the shortest distance away from England and closest to the German border? The high command chose the latter option primarily for two compelling reasons. First, Adolf Hitler had always believed Calais was a target, and, second, the Allies had leaked misinformation to the Germans that convinced them that General George Patton, the brilliant commander of the 3rd Army, was compiling a force to strike across the Channel at the Pas de Calais. The Germans' choice proved costly, since a rapid response from the main German contingent quite possibly could have thwarted the Allied landings at Normandy.

D Day

Although the first of the now-famous beach landings that characterize D day (the military designation for the day of the landings) took place at 6:30 A.M. on June 6, 1944, the operation actually began six hours earlier. Several miles inland from the Normandy beaches, U.S. and British planes were dropping paratroops and detaching gliders filled with men. The U.S. 101st and 82nd Airborne Divisions dropped behind the planned beachhead designated as "Utah" on the eastern edge of the Cotentin Peninsula. Because of the poor visibility, several units overshot their drop zones. Many of these paratroopers plunged into blackness and landed in the swamps and flooded fields in the region. Some of the unfortunate, weighed down by packs and rifles, drowned before they could shed their equipment. The ones that survived the fall were scattered far from the other units in their battalions. Despite the paratroops' scattered deployment and the stiff resistance of some Germans, who fired antiaircraft weapons and machine guns at the helpless Americans in the air or tangled in their chutes on the ground, the Americans succeeded in causing confusion. The Germans were caught off guard, and they were unsure of how large an attacking force they were facing. Some were not even sure it was an invasion. As author Stephen E. Ambrose relates, "The Germans could not tell whether this was the invasion or a series of scattered raids or a diversion to precede landings in the Pas-de-Calais or a supply op-

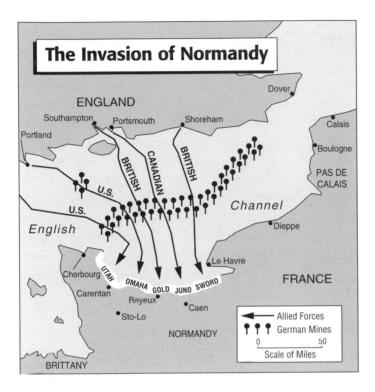

The Invasion of Normandy

ENGLAND

Dover

Southampton   Portsmouth   Shoreham

Portland

Calais

Boulogne

PAS DE
CALAIS

BRITISH   CANADIAN   BRITISH

U.S.

U.S.

Channel

English

Dieppe

UTAH   OMAHA   GOLD   JUNO   SWORD

Le Havre

Cherbourg

Carentan

Bayeux

Sto-Lo

Caen

FRANCE

NORMANDY

Allied Forces
German Mines
0   50
Scale of Miles

BRITTANY

eration to the [French] Resistance."[45] By daylight of June 6, fragments of American units who did link up were in control of the strategic town of Ste.-Mère-Église and had successfully repelled a German counterattack.

The British paratroops fared a bit better. The 6th Airborne descended in gliders, which kept their forces together. They came down to the east of "Sword" beach, near the city of Caen. Their objectives were to capture vital bridges near Caen and to eliminate gun batteries at Merville that overlooked the Sword beachhead. The bridges were seized relatively easily, although holding them against the 12th SS Panzer Division proved costly. The assault on the Merville batteries, however, began badly. The gliders carrying the demolition equipment and flamethrowers (necessities when attacking cement bunkers) were blown off course and never made it to the assembly point. Also, Lieutenant Colonel Terence Otway had not collected all of his men before time constraints forced him to attack. The batteries were scheduled to be shelled by Allied naval forces at 5:30 A.M., and it was already 4:30 A.M. when Otway had reached the staging point. With his handful of men, he assaulted the positions. Though they took heavy casualties, they succeeded in destroying the guns. Ironically, they were much lower-caliber guns than Allied intelligence had reported (therefore less of a threat), and after the British paratroops evacuated the area, the Germans returned quickly and repaired two of the guns, which ended up firing on Sword beach.

Softening Up

The Allied commanders knew the beach landings would not be easy. Since the British, Canadians, and Americans coming ashore would be met by defenders in better positions, the navy and air force were ordered to "soften up" the area by directing their efforts against the cement bunkers. All through the early-morning hours of June 6, waves of Allied heavy bombers were sent to expend their payloads on the coastal

The Bannon Bomb

In *The Invasion of Normandy*, author David Pietrusza relates a bit of British ingenuity. Each British paratrooper in Normandy carried with him a variety of deadly weapons. One of his favorites was the so-called Bannon Bomb, an explosive device invented in the North African campaign of 1942. It was not devised by a team of highly trained munitions experts or in any top-secret laboratory or arsenal. It was created in the field by Lieutenant Jock Bannon of the British 1st Parachute Brigade.

The Bannon Bomb was the essence of simplicity, and, despite its light weight, it packed a deadly punch. The Bannon Bomb consisted of two pounds of plastic explosive (with an igniting device in the middle) that was tightly packed into a black bag. The bag would then be thrown at a German tank. The explosion was capable of damaging the tank's steel outer shell and even possibly ripping off a portion of its revolving gun turret.

One disadvantage of the Bannon Bomb was its short life span. This was not because of any design flaw but because resourceful British and American paratroopers soon discovered they could conveniently break off small pieces of the explosive and use them to start campfires. The result was a fighting force well supplied with piping hot coffee or tea but with increasingly smaller Bannon Bombs at its disposal to hurl at enemy tanks.

defenses. Unfortunately, the sky was quite dark and the bomber pilots had difficulty seeing their targets. Unable to locate the ground along Utah beach, the pilots assigned to harry that position decided not to drop their bombs. Those missions that did drop bombs met with equally poor results. For example, the last wave of 8th Air Force bombers to strike before the landings was ordered to delay the release of its bombs to avoid having them explode near the landing forces coming ashore. The thirty-second delay, however, caused most of the ordnance to fall far inland, well behind the defenses. The bombings along the coast had accomplished nothing.

Naval ships could fire with much more accuracy, and they had the advantage of not opening up until 6:00 A.M., when daybreak provided enough light. Yet even many of the naval spotters misjudged the range. Shells from the 12- and 14-inch guns of the three U.S. battleships fell far inland. The numerous destroyers on hand were more accurate, but their smaller-caliber guns failed to penetrate the thick cement pillboxes. At 6:30 A.M., when the first Americans hit Utah and Omaha beaches, the German defenders were alert, and, more significant, their positions were untouched.

The Atlantic Wall

The Atlantic Wall signified not only the elaborate string of pillboxes and bunkers but also the entire defensive measures concocted by the Germans to hold up an invasion fleet. The German plan had never been to deter a landing. General Erwin Rommel, who was in charge of organizing the defenses, knew he did not have enough men or weapons to keep the Allies from reaching the beaches. The German air force had been decimated by Allied precision bombing, so air cover could not terrorize the ships or landing craft at sea. Rommel counted on his beach defenses to slow the

Allied progress inland until the infantry and armored divisions in the area could be summoned to the correct landing spot and crush the beachhead.

The German defenses did not begin at the beaches; they extended out into the surf. The Germans had planted posts angled toward an oncoming fleet all along the water route to shore. Atop the posts were Teller mines set to detonate on contact. At low tide, the posts were visible, but at high tide, when the landing craft would make their runs for the beach, the mines rested just below the waterline, waiting to knock out unwary craft. Closer to the shoreline were obstacles—such as crossed railroad ties—intended to slow the progress of the landing craft and give defenders time to train their guns on the incoming assault boats. Once ashore, the Allied attackers were without cover along the three-hundred-yard stretches of sandy beach. Mines dotted the beach and blocked off paths inward, thus confining the invasion to certain areas where the Germans had targeted their weapons. While working forward to the seawall (the inland edge of the sandy beach), the disembarked troops were subject to machine-gun fire from trenches and pillboxes on the high ground. Also housed in hardened bunkers, a handful of 75-mm and 88-mm guns were also trained to harass the infantry and knock out any armor the Allies could get ashore. At the seawall, the landing

The remains of German obstacles at Normandy can still be seen today. These posts were once armed with mines to destroy Allied landing craft.

troops were generally protected from direct fire, but explosive shells lobbed behind the wall could still send fragments into the air, killing or maiming any unfortunates. Because of this, the troops couldn't stay at the seawall for long. They had to move inland to secure the beachhead. In anticipation, the Germans had strung rows of concertina wire just beyond the seawall to further slow the advance inland. The layers of these various defenses were strong at some beaches and weak at others, but all in all they proved formidable.

The weak link in General Rommel's strategy was the quality of many of his troops and their arms. Even the men in the defenses knew they were unfit and underprepared. One officer commented, "We were conscious that neither our men nor our tanks were good enough."[46] The Germans had been fighting so long and losing so many young men to combat that the average age of the German defender was thirty-one, or six years older than his American counterpart. Many of these men were second-class troops, those Germans unfit for frontline duty. As historians Donald M. Goldstein, Katherine V. Dillon, and Michael Wenger humorously note, "One whole division in Normandy was composed entirely of men with stomach ailments."[47] Equally disappointing were the foreign-born "volunteers" who had been inducted into the German army when their native lands had been conquered. Thus, instead of meeting the crack resistance of hardy German fanatics, the Allies were commonly faced with Poles and Russians who were more inclined to fire their guns once or twice and then surrender.

Most of the troops defending Normandy were unfit for frontline duty. This older German soldier is using a cane.

Of course, not all the German defenders were poor fighters, but one problem or another hampered many of the divisions. Most were undermanned; some divisions could only muster two regiments of troops instead of the normal three. Since Allied air attacks over the preceding months had destroyed anything traveling the roads around the beaches, many defending units lacked mobility, slowing their own progress in reaching and occupying the coastal defenses. Of the many bunkers and pillboxes, several were either unfinished or lacked armament. Those that did contain weapons usually were fitted with captured guns from French, Polish, Russian, and Yugoslav campaigns. These were generally of lesser caliber than the standard German field pieces, and they each required different ammunition, which complicated the routing of the correct ammo supply to the appropriate bunker. Thus, the Allied troops coming ashore had some advantages unbeknownst to them, though that did not mean the landings were without peril.

An LCVP packed with GIs begins its run to the beach. The mines planted by the Germans would cripple many of these landing craft.

Utah

At 3:45 in the morning of June 6, the American soldiers, who had been practicing beach landings in Britain for the past few months, were setting off from the troop ships that lay twelve miles off the Normandy coast. Most of the men were packed into LCTs (landing craft, tank) or LCVPs (landing craft, vehicle, personnel) that sped toward the shore at roughly 10 knots, meaning the ride to the beach would take three hours. The LCVPs, the smallest of the landing craft, were tublike conveyances that could hold thirty-six men or small vehicles and ordnance such as jeeps and antitank guns. The LCTs were landing craft with larger capacities to carry tanks and larger guns to the beaches. Although the men aboard huddled below the protective wall of these ships, the boats were vulnerable to ar-

tillery and antitank shells from the German shore batteries. Miraculously, few of the LCVPs and their larger kin were struck in this manner; more were plagued with mechanical difficulties that left the boats and men swamped at sea than were damaged by enemy fire. The Teller mines attached to the poles under the surf, however, did cripple many craft, but occasionally the crews of these vessels were able to disembark intact and swim the remaining distance to the shore.

The American troops approaching the Cotentin Peninsula at Utah beach were fortunate in many ways. The paratroops of the 82nd and 101st Airborne Divisions had successfully tied up Germans behind the beachhead, leaving the beach defenders with no reinforcements. The airborne units had also

American soldiers wade ashore at Utah Beach. The troops landed at a relatively undefended sector and suffered few casualties.

captured some artillery batteries inland that could have shelled the beach area mercilessly. But perhaps the most favorable news was that the landing craft had missed the designated landing zone. They had driven off course and brought the men ashore to the south of the intended target. Goldstein, Dillon, and Wenger assert, "Providence—or luck—had moved the landing site from a heavily defended sector to one that was almost unprotected."[48] Although a few landing craft were lost to the tempestuous sea and one struck a mine, the majority of the American force swarmed ashore unabated. Recognizing that his men were not where they were intended to land, General Theodore Roosevelt Jr. weighed his options and reportedly exclaimed, "We'll start the war from right here." Whether factual or not, the decision was important because a second wave of men would be landing to the

north if not diverted to the new beachhead. But the order was given and the men and tanks pushed up from the beach. Within one hour the entire beachhead was secure and heavy equipment and tanks were being unloaded for the drive inland. It was a textbook landing; there were only 197 casualties of the 23,000 that came ashore on the first day. The bulk of the American invasion units quickly headed to make contact with the airborne infantry that was still holding back the Germans just a few miles away.

Omaha

Unlike the Utah operation, the landings at the Omaha beachhead were disastrous. High cliffs dotted with pillboxes commanded parts of the beach. Once ashore, the Americans were completely vulnerable to the German weapons pointing down at them. One German soldier witnessing the incoming troops remarked, "They must be crazy. Are they going to swim ashore? Right under our muzzles?"[49] The defenders were also not the anticipated second-line troops that manned most defenses on the Atlantic Wall; the crack 352nd Infantry Division had been moved into the area just a week prior to the invasion. The Americans would be met with stiff resistance from nearly impenetrable positions. Speaking of the 16th Infantry Regiment landing, Stephen Ambrose describes the slaughter that ensued: "The American infantry struggled ashore with no support whatsoever. Casualties were extremely heavy, especially in the water and in the 200 meters or so of open beach. As with the 116th to the right, for the 16th Regiment first and second waves D-Day was more reminiscent of an infantry charge across no-man's-land at the Somme in World War I

than a typical World War II action."[50] The casualty rate would be so high (more than two thousand men), the beachhead was quickly nicknamed "Bloody Omaha."

The problems at Omaha started early. The American admiral in charge of the naval ships supporting the landings refused to bring his gunboats within eight miles of the beach because he feared being hit by shore batteries. As a result, the prelanding gunfire from these vessels was imprecise and completely ineffective. The seas were also particularly rough at Omaha, swamping many landing craft as they traveled toward shore. The waves also flooded the new amphibious tanks that had been designed for this mission. These M4A3 Shermans, fitted with flotation collars and tall vent stacks to keep water out of the engine ports, were intended to move through calm waters; the

Under heavy fire from crack German infantrymen, GIs crawl between beach obstacles at "Bloody Omaha."

high surf they encountered capsized a majority. Only five made it to the shore to support the infantry.

Once the LCTs and LCVPs came toward the shore, they were met by accurate defensive fire. Rommel had personally supervised the organization of defenses. As Stephen Ambrose describes, "He laid out the firing positions at angles to the beach to cover the tidal flat and beach shelf with crossing fire, plunging fire, and grazing fire, from all types of weapons. He prepared artillery positions along the cliffs at either end of the beach, capable of delivering enfilade [raking] fire from 88s all across Omaha."[51] The German guns coupled with the turbulent seas proved to be a formidable combination. In many units only two-thirds of the landing craft ever touched the beach. Upon unloading, the infantry were raked by machine-gun fire. It was not uncommon for entire companies of men to take 50 percent casualties as they clambered out of the ships. Most men dropped into the water for protection but then had to swim to shore. The lucky ones made it to the seawall and huddled for cover, although as Max Hastings notes, "some companies' survivors took 45 minutes to struggle even that far from the waterline."[52] And once there, the soldiers realized that the wall provided little protection from the Germans looking downward from the cliffs above.

Taking the cliffs was an obvious necessity to keep the tenuous beachhead intact. The U.S. Army rangers were given the mission of seizing the high ground and knock-ing out six 155-mm guns in protective casements above. They had ladders and rocket-propelled grappling hooks to assist in the climb up the near-vertical cliff faces. At Pointe du Hoc, they made their ascent. The well-positioned Germans cut many down as they struggled up the terrain, typically weaponless because of the need to hold on to ropes or the bare earth. Several men died while still suspended from their climbing ropes. It was a grisly scene. Intelligence reports had warned of the dangers of attempting to scale the cliffs. One staff officer had concluded, "Three old women with brooms could keep the Rangers from climbing that cliff."[53] But slowly the rangers moved upward and pressed their attack, helped by renewed naval gunfire that kept the defenders at bay. In teams of two or three men, the rangers performed acts of bravery, eliminating pillboxes and bunkers with grenades and satchel charges filled with TNT. Ironically, the guns they were sent to eliminate turned out to be telephone poles disguised to look like cannon. The real weapons had been removed recently, probably because of the preinvasion bombardment. With Pointe du Hoc in American hands, the Allies could begin moving up the beach. The rangers, however, had paid the price. Only 90 of the original 225 rangers were still fit for combat by day's end.

Despite the reprieve granted by the rangers, the men advancing up the beach were stymied because the paths off the beach had been blocked by obstacles placed by the German army. In some cases, wooden

The Funnies

In *The Invasion of Normandy*, David Pietrusza notes some of the ungainly vehicles that the Allies employed to overcome the difficulties of assaulting the Atlantic Wall. The invaders needed mobile armored firepower on the Normandy beaches, but landing tanks in storm-tossed waters and on rocky beaches was no easy task.

The 1942 Dieppe invasion had failed in part because of a deficiency of armored units, and Prime Minister Churchill wanted to avoid the same mistake. Accordingly, he ordered Major General Percy C. S. Hobart to develop tanks that could surmount virtually any landing difficulty. His new tanks were very unorthodox in design, and the men who operated them dubbed the strange and humorous-looking vehicles "the Funnies."

The DD (duplex drive) tanks were originally not Hobart's idea, but he perfected them. Hobart's versions were driven by two propellers at the rear (hence duplex drive) and carried a flotation collar that rose up from the hull to surround the turret and engine deck to keep water from entering the vehicle. The collar had to be deflated before the tank's gun could operate. The Americans mockingly nicknamed the DD Shermans "Donald Ducks," but that did not stop them from using them on D day and wishing they had more.

Engineer units possessed most of the Funnies because these units were given the task of getting the men off the soft beaches quickly, which meant crossing the soft sand, plowing through minefields, crossing difficult terrain features, and eliminating the enemy pillboxes. Hobart's "bobbin" tank was a modified British Churchill with a treadmill of mesh matting that unrolled in the tank's path as it moved forward. The carpet of material allowed the vehicle to move up soft, slippery beaches quickly. The Sherman flail tank cleared minefields with its lengths of chain spun outward from a rotating drum affixed to arms extending from the front hull. The British called their version "the Crab." The various AVRE (armoured vehicle royal engineer) were of use farther inland. One, another modified Churchill, carried bridging sections that could be laid over ditches or streams to keep the armored columns moving forward. A second AVRE Churchill carried a Petard demolition projectile, essentially a large-caliber mortar round that was capable of breaching enemy bunkers and pillboxes.

Hobart's Funnies may have been awkward in appearance, but they worked well on the Normandy beaches. And the Germans who saw them coming straight at them on D day certainly found nothing to laugh at.

and cement walls plugged the access roads that led inland. Engineer units were supposed to clear these roadblocks with bulldozers and explosives, but much of the required munitions and vehicles were adrift in the water or destroyed on the beaches. And the engineer squads themselves were decimated. Grabbing whatever explosives were left, untrained and inexperienced GIs, with the support of the remaining engineers, seized the initiative. One device, the bangalore torpedo, was a long hoselike contraption that was designed to be pushed under the obstacle and then detonated. The tube sections that comprised the bangalore torpedo, however, were meant to be affixed before the device was used. Instead, the infantrymen ran into the open, braved enemy fire, and tied the tubes together in a piecemeal progression toward the roadblocks.

Despite the casualties among the men busily assembling the weapon, the bangalore torpedoes and other explosives worked. The obstacles were destroyed, and the roads up the beaches were cleared. It was a telling moment because a second wave of landing craft was scheduled to follow the first assault onto the beaches; without freedom to move inland, the new arrivals and the six-hour veterans would be congested on the beachhead, easy targets for German artillery. The situation was so dire that General Omar Bradley, in charge of the invasion forces, seriously considered abandoning Omaha and shifting the reserves to another beach. But the individual acts of heroism and the improvisational skills of the American combat soldiers prevailed; by 1:30 P.M.—after seven hours of murderous fire and situational calamities—the troops were moving inland and the beachhead was secure.

Sword and Gold

At 7:25 A.M., the British invasion forces began coming ashore at Sword and "Gold" beaches. Sword was the easternmost of the designated beachheads, and it was expected to be the most heavily defended. When the British troops hit the beach, they fell into a hail of deadly machine-gun fire. Whole units were torn apart. It appeared to be another Omaha-like tragedy. However, the British had suc-

cessfully landed five Sherman Flail tanks on Sword beach. These unique vehicles were Sherman tanks equipped with a rotating drum extended from arms on the front of the tank. Affixed to the drum were several lengths of chain that spun furiously when the drum was operated. The devices were designed to clear minefields on the beaches, and they worked exceptionally well. The chains would set off the mines at a safe distance from the vehicle and clear a path up the beach. The tanks also had their normal 75-mm guns, which blasted the German positions.

With this support, the infantry could move quickly inland. The way was still treacherous, but the uncommon valor of

The Utah and Omaha beachheads secure, reinforcements and equipment pour into Normandy and move inland.

the British troops was apparent at all times. Lord Simon Lovat, for example, had promised the 6th Airborne, which had eliminated the Merville battery, that his commando unit would link up with the beleaguered paratroops by noon. Not wanting to go back on his word, he ordered his company's bagpiper to play some Scottish Highland music to urge the men forward. The strategy worked, and his men surged forward to face Germans who were effectively stunned by the curious noise that filled the air. Lovat's men and the airborne troops linked up rather quickly, though the commando leader was forced to apologize for being "a couple of minutes late."

Gold beach was situated just to the east of Omaha. It was well defended, and the emplacements had not been damaged by the preceding waves of bombers and naval gunfire. The landing was thus troubled from the start. Most units of the British 50th Division were plagued by accurate German artillery fire. Of the sixteen LCVPs belonging to one commando unit, four were sunk outright and another eleven were so badly damaged they could not return to their mother ship. In addition to the losses that had already occurred, the tides at Gold beach were rising rapidly and the British engineers had not had an opportunity to dismantle all of the mines affixed to the underwater obstacles. The British had new duplex drive (or DD) tanks, like the American amphibious Shermans, that were waiting to "swim" to shore in support of the infantry, but fear of the undiscovered mines was keeping them at bay. When the situation seemed the most precarious, the tanks were allowed to proceed blindly through the surf. The tanks made it to shore, and with their assistance the infantry was able to overcome the surprisingly few defenders. By day's end, the British had pushed six miles inland, thwarted a German counterattack, and were situated less than a mile from the city of Bayeux.

Juno

Stuck between Gold and Sword beaches, "Juno" beach was the only beach assigned to the Canadian army. The Canadians had suffered a complete disaster when they tried to stage a landing at Dieppe, France, in 1942. The raid was designed to be a test case for a larger amphibious assault; its goals were merely to see how the Germans would react in the face of a beach landing in the west. The mission failed utterly because of the lack of cohesion between air, sea, and ground forces. The Canadians on the beaches were cut down or captured almost immediately. Now they feared that Juno would be a repeat of the Dieppe catastrophe. But time had favored the Canadian army; its troops were well seasoned after victories in North Africa and Italy. The German defenders, on the other hand, were a combination of the very young and the very old—the bottom of Germany's barrel of reserves. The Canadians were also putting roughly twenty-four hundred men and seventy-six tanks against barely four hundred German troops whose artillery was primarily horse-drawn. Still, the preinvasion naval bombardment and air attacks had accomplished little for the Canadians. And once ashore, the troops were stuck in a four-mile-wide stretch of minefield.

The Canadians were late in hitting the beaches, and they were almost immediately pinned down. Like the British, what helped the Canadian infantry was the arrival of their DD tanks. Some Canadian troops reported seeing German defenders standing agape as the amphibious tanks rolled up from the sea and started shelling the bunkers. In comparison with the other beaches, the Canadians fared well. Allied command had anticipated that the assault on Juno might suffer two thousand men dead or wounded, but by the end of June 6, the Canadians were in control of the beachhead after taking only half that many casualties. The Canadians had avoided another Dieppe and through determination had driven farther inland than any other amphibious force on the five beachheads.

Aftermath

The D day invasion gave the Allies their foothold in northern Europe. Although they had made landings in Italy to the south, the Normandy beaches were much closer to the heart of Nazi Germany. It was hoped that by cutting across the north, the Allies could reach Germany more quickly and bring about a resolution to the war. The German high command, on the other hand, had misjudged the beach landings. Adolf Hitler believed that the Normandy landings were a diversion and that the main assault was yet to come at the Pas de Calais, much closer to the German homeland. In anticipation for this invasion that never came, Hitler refused to release several elite panzer divisions to stem the tide in Normandy. Many historians believe that a quick decisive counterattack by the crack German tank divisions bottled up in Calais could have overwhelmed the beachheads in short order. But it was not to be. Only after the Allies continued to pour men and matériel into the Normandy region did Hitler allow some (not all) of the panzer divisions to move into Normandy. The effort was too little and too late. The Allies had half a million men in the area just eleven days after the landings. They had to contend with stubborn German resistance from frontline troops, but eventually the Allies pushed out of the region and began the slow march toward Berlin.

☆ Notes ☆

Introduction: Improving Modern Warfare

1. Chris Bishop, ed., *The Encyclopedia of Weapons of World War II*. New York: Barnes and Noble, 1998, p. 7.

Chapter 1: The Tank: Armored Blitzkrieg

2. Ward Rutherford, *Blitzkrieg 1940*. New York: Gallery Books, 1979, p. 12.
3. *Tanks and Weapons of World War II*. New York: Beekman House, 1973, p. 10.
4. Hans von Luck, *Panzer Commander*. New York: Praeger, 1989, p. 62.
5. Denis Bishop and Christopher Ellis, *Vehicles at War*. Cranbury, NJ: A. S. Barnes, 1979, p. 123.
6. *Tanks and Weapons of World War II*, p. 42.
7. *Tanks and Weapons of World War II*, p. 107.
8. Omar Nelson Bradley, *A Soldier's Story*. New York: Henry Holt, 1951, p. 41.
9. Quoted in Earl Frederick Ziemke, *The Soviet Juggernaut*. Alexandria, VA: Time-Life Books, 1980, p. 133.

Chapter 2: The U-Boat: War in the Atlantic

10. Richard Humble, *Undersea Warfare*. Secaucus, NJ: Chartwell Books, 1981, p. 65.

11. Richard Compton-Hall, *The Underwater War 1939–1945*. Dorset, England: Blandford Press, 1982, p. 65.
12. Donald Macintyre, *U-boat Killer: A Stirring Account of Destroyer Action in the Battle of the Atlantic*. Annapolis, MD: Naval Institute Press, 1956, p. 50.
13. Peter Cremer, *U-boat Commander: A Periscope View of the Battle of the Atlantic*. Annapolis, MD: Naval Institute Press, 1984, p. 59.
14. Quoted in Joseph A. Skiera, ed., *Aircraft Carriers in Peace and War*. New York: Franklin Watts, 1965, p. 72.
15. Cremer, *U-boat Commander*, p. 132.
16. Quoted in Edwin P. Hoyt, *U-boats: A Pictorial History*. New York: McGraw-Hill, 1987, p. 198.

Chapter 3: Flattops: The Carrier War in the Pacific

17. Clark G. Reynolds, *The Carrier War*. Alexandria, VA: Time-Life Books, 1982, p. 49.
18. Quoted in Reynolds, *The Carrier War*, p. 61.
19. Harry A. Gailey, *The War in the Pacific: From Pearl Harbor to Tokyo Bay*. Novato, CA: Presidio Press, 1995, p. 147.
20. Donald Macintyre, *Aircraft Carriers: The*

Majestic Weapon. New York: Ballantine Books, 1968, p. 85.

21. Macintyre, *Aircraft Carriers*, p. 85.

22. Harold L. Buell, *Dauntless Helldivers: A Dive-Bomber Pilot's Epic Story of the Carrier Battles.* New York: Orion Books, 1991, p. 82.

23. Quoted in Buell, *Dauntless Helldivers*, p. 86.

24. Quoted in Reynolds, *The Carrier War*, p. 128.

25. David C. Cooke, *Fighter Planes.* New York: G. P. Putnam's Sons, 1958, p. 42.

26. Quoted in Reynolds, *The Carrier War*, p. 170.

Chapter 4: The Fighter Plane: Duels in the Sky

27. Quoted in Alexander McKee, *Strike from the Sky: The Story of the Battle of Britain.* Boston: Little, Brown, 1960, p. 29.

28. Quoted in McKee, *Strike from the Sky,* p. 29.

29. Norman Franks, *Battle of Britain.* New York: Galahad Books, 1981, p. 30.

30. Franks, *Battle of Britain*, p. 49.

31. Quoted in Cooke, *Fighter Planes*, p. 44.

32. Quoted in Stuart Leuthner and Oliver Jensen, *High Honor: Recollections by Men and Women of World War II Aviation.* Washington, DC: Smithsonian Institution, 1989.

33. Quoted in William Newby Grant, *P-51 Mustang.* Secaucus, NJ: Chartwell Books, 1980, p. 22.

34. Heinz Knoke, *I Flew for the Führer.* New York: Henry Holt, 1990, p. 201.

Chapter 5: The Bomber: The Air War over Germany

35. Quoted in Max Hastings, *Bomber Command.* New York: Dial Press, 1979, p. 41.

36. Quoted in Hastings, *Bomber Command,* p. 77.

37. Quoted in Hastings, *Bomber Command,* p. 116.

38. Lord Douglas of Kirtleside, *Combat and Command: The Story of an Airman in Two World Wars.* New York: Simon and Schuster, 1966, p. 571.

39. Quoted in Gerald Astor, *The Mighty Eighth: The Air War in Europe As Told by the Men Who Fought It.* New York, Donald I. Fine Books, 1997, p. 43.

40. Quoted in Astor, *The Mighty Eighth*, p. 45.

41. Quoted in Alvin M. Josephy Jr., ed., *The American Heritage History of Flight.* New York: American Heritage, 1962, p. 331.

42. Quoted in Studs Terkel, *"The Good War": An Oral History of World War II.* New York: New Press, 1984, p. 208.

43. Hastings, *Bomber Command*, p. 228.

44. Quoted in Josephy, *The American Heritage History of Flight*, p. 334.

Chapter 6: D Day: Everything Put to the Test

45. Stephen E. Ambrose, *D-Day June 6, 1944: The Climactic Battle of World War II.* New York: Simon and Schuster, 1994, p. 216.

46. Quoted in Max Hastings, *Overlord: D-Day and the Battle for Normandy.* New York:

Simon and Schuster, 1984, p. 65.

47. Donald M. Goldstein, Katherine V. Dillon, and J. Michael Wenger, *D-Day Normandy: The Story and Photographs.* McLean, VA: Brassey's, 1994, p. 18.

48. Goldstein et al., *D-Day Normandy*, p. 98.

49. Quoted in Hastings, *Overlord*, p. 89.

50. Ambrose, *D-Day June 6, 1944*, p. 346.

51. Ambrose, *D-Day June 6, 1944*, p. 321.

52. Hastings, *Overlord*, p. 91.

53. Quoted in Goldstein et al., *D-Day Normandy*, p. 92.

⋆ For Further Reading ⋆

Denis Bishop and Christopher Ellis, *Vehicles at War*. Cranbury, NJ: A. S. Barnes, 1979. A basic account of the evolution of military vehicles from World War II through the 1970s. It is filled with hand-drawn images of the vehicles discussed, and the descriptions are not overly technical.

Richard Compton-Hall, *The Underwater War 1939–1945*. Dorset, England: Blandford Press, 1982. An excellent volume on submarine warfare in World War II. There are interesting discussions of tactics and methods of attack, and the book is filled with photos and graphics.

David C. Cooke, *Fighter Planes*. New York: G. P. Putnam's Sons, 1958. A short, introductory volume on many fighter planes throughout the modern era. A competent starting point for beginners.

Len Deighton, *Battle of Britain*. London: George Rainbird Limited, 1980. An excellent introductory volume on the Battle of Britain. This book offers a good combination of text and visuals.

Donald M. Goldstein, Katherine V. Dillon, and J. Michael Wenger, *D-Day Normandy: The Story and Photographs*. McLean, VA: Brassey's, 1994. An excellent overview of Normandy. Though the text is brief, an entire section is devoted to the weapons used in the battle. The book also contains wonderful photos.

Edwin P. Hoyt, *U-boats: A Pictorial History*. New York: McGraw-Hill, 1987. As the title states, this book is primarily devoted to interesting, and perhaps rare, photos of life aboard German U-boats. There is some useful contextual information provided in brief chapter introductions.

Edward Jablonski, *A Pictorial History of the World War II Years*. Garden City, NY: Doubleday, 1977. A good photo history of the war. The color photographs are of the most interest.

David Pietrusza, *The Invasion of Normandy*. San Diego: Lucent Books, 1996. A concise history of the preparation for and execution of the Normandy landings.

Clark G. Reynolds, *The Carrier War*. Alexandria, VA: Time-Life Books, 1982. One of Time-Life's attractive books, this overview of the carrier war in the Pacific is engaging as well as informative. Many graphics and photos support the text.

Earle Rice Jr., *The Battle of Midway*. San Diego: Lucent Books, 1996. A good account of the exciting action around Midway. Photos, maps, and sidebars accompany the main text.

☆ Works Consulted ☆

Stephen E. Ambrose, *D-Day June 6, 1944: The Climactic Battle of World War II*. New York: Simon and Schuster, 1994. Ambrose is one of America's most popular historians. Like most of his works, this book is informative and riveting, primarily because of his collection and presentation of eyewitness accounts.

Gerald Astor, *The Mighty Eighth: The Air War in Europe As Told by the Men Who Fought It*. New York: Donald I. Fine Books, 1997. Engrossing account of the 8th Air Force and their missions over Germany. Many firsthand accounts make the book a lively read.

Chris Bishop, ed., *The Encyclopedia of Weapons of World War II*. New York: Barnes and Noble, 1998. Quite a good but hefty encyclopedia of various weapons used in the war; includes everything from handheld weapons to planes, ships, and rockets.

Omar Nelson Bradley, *A Soldier's Story*. New York: Henry Holt, 1951. Bradley was one of the most famous U.S. generals of the war. He served in North Africa and Italy and commanded the American forces at Normandy. His autobiography of the war years is a classic.

Eric M. Brown, *Duels in the Sky: World War II Naval Aircraft in Combat*. Annapolis, MD: Airlife, 1988. Famed British test pilot Eric Brown creates an interesting book that discusses the strengths and weaknesses of specific planes when matched against each other in hypothetical duels. Added to these "duels" are brief accounts of major battles involving the various planes.

Harold L. Buell, *Dauntless Helldivers: A Dive-Bomber Pilot's Epic Story of the Carrier Battles*. New York: Orion Books, 1991. Buell, a former Dauntless dive-bomber pilot, wrote a fascinating firsthand account of his experiences as an airman aboard several U.S. carriers. The book is filled with interesting anecdotes and Buell's interpretation of key events in the Pacific Theater.

Ronald W. Clark, *The Role of the Bomber*. New York: Thomas Y. Crowell, 1977. A useful book that explores the roles bomber planes have played in many actions from the 1910s to the 1970s. Both tactical and strategic bombers are discussed.

Peter Cremer, *U-boat Commander: A Periscope View of the Battle of the Atlantic*. Annapolis, MD: Naval Institute Press, 1984. An excellent and riveting account of the Battle of the Atlantic from a U-boat commander who served one of the longest, most successful tours of duty in the German submarine forces.

Lord Douglas of Kirtleside, *Combat and Command: The Story of an Airman in Two World Wars.* New York: Simon and Schuster, 1966. Lord Douglas served as a pilot in the First World War and became the head of Britain's fighter command in the Second World War. With his unique perspective as an airman, he relates a lengthy story of the Royal Air Force and the command decisions made throughout World War II.

George Forty, *Tank Action: From the Great War to the Gulf.* London: Greenwich Editions, 1996. British historian George Forty has written several books on tanks. This one is a collection of short anecdotal pieces covering specific battles. The book discusses engagements from the First World War through the Gulf War.

Norman Franks, *Battle of Britain.* New York: Galahad Books, 1981. A short introductory book on the Battle of Britain; good firsthand quotes garnered from participants in the air campaign.

Roger A. Freeman, *B-17 Fortress at War.* New York: Charles Scribner's Sons, 1977. One of Freeman's many books detailing specific combat airplanes. The volume is filled with discussion of the advent, design, workings, and missions of the Flying Fortress. It has many anecdotes and a wealth of detailed pictures.

———, *Mustang at War.* Garden City, NY: Doubleday, 1974. Another of Freeman's aviation books, this volume covers the evolution of the Mustang from its introductory service with the British through its mastery of the air under the U.S. Army Air Force. Plenty of technical detail and pictures give an accurate account of the Mustang in military service.

Harry A. Gailey, *The War in the Pacific: From Pearl Harbor to Tokyo Bay.* Novato, CA: Presidio Press, 1995. A broad overview of the Pacific War. Gailey is capable of fleshing out the big picture, but the text lacks any firsthand accounts or lively anecdotes.

William Newby Grant, *P-51 Mustang.* Secaucus, NJ: Chartwell Books, 1980. Written by a lecturer at the Royal Military Academy, this book is a basic overview of the P-51's development. It has many diagrams and photos but lacks many anecdotes from pilots who flew the famous planes.

Max Hastings, *Bomber Command.* New York: Dial Press, 1979. British historian Max Hastings listened to many firsthand accounts from the bomber pilots as well as some from their superiors in bomber command to create this thorough discussion of Britain's major contributions to the air campaign over Germany.

———, *Overlord: D-Day and the Battle for Normandy.* New York: Simon and Schuster, 1984. Hastings' account of the Normandy invasion. As thoroughgoing as most other texts on the operation.

Edwin P. Hoyt, *The Death of the U-boats.* New York: McGraw-Hill, 1988. Good introduction to the U-boat story, from early success to final defeat.

Richard Humble, *Undersea Warfare.* Secaucus, NJ: Chartwell Books, 1981. An overview of the evolution of underwater warfare from the Revolutionary War to the advent of nuclear submarines. The Second World War section is fairly detailed, but the overall picture of submarine warfare is impressive.

Alvin M. Josephy Jr., ed., *The American Heritage History of Flight*. New York: American Heritage, 1962. A collection of essays and photos detailing the advent of flight and the many roles aircraft have played. Some useful information on combat airplanes.

Heinz Knoke, *I Flew for the Führer*. New York: Henry Holt, 1990. Excerpts from Knoke's diary detail his service in the Luftwaffe.

Stuart Leuthner and Oliver Jensen, *High Honor: Recollections by Men and Women of World War II Aviation*. Washington, DC: Smithsonian Institution, 1989. As the title indicates, this volume is a collection of anecdotes from veterans of the war. Multiple perspectives give a unique view of everything from the extraordinary to the mundane.

Hans von Luck, *Panzer Commander*. New York: Praeger, 1989. Written by the commander of the 21st Panzer Division, Luck's memoir is an extremely interesting view of the war from the German perspective.

Donald Macintyre, *Aircraft Carriers: The Majestic Weapon*. New York: Ballantine Books, 1968. Part of Ballantine's Illustrated History of World War II, this volume on aircraft carriers charts the development of the vessels and their major campaigns in both the Pacific and Atlantic. A thorough overview with encyclopedia-style maps and drawings.

———, *U-boat Killer: A Stirring Account of Destroyer Action in the Battle of the Atlantic*. Annapolis, MD: Naval Institute Press, 1956. Macintyre's own account of his work aboard a destroyer escort in the Atlantic.

Alexander McKee, *Strike from the Sky: The Story of the Battle of Britain*. Boston: Little, Brown, 1960. A thorough and interesting account of the Battle of Britain. Filled with firsthand accounts from British and German pilots.

Samuel Eliot Morison, *The Two-Ocean War: A Short History of the United States Navy in the Second World War*. Boston: Little, Brown, 1963. Although billed as a "short history," Morison's book is a thick, well-detailed account of naval combat in the Pacific and Atlantic. It has a very concise account of the action at Midway and the Coral Sea.

Gordon W. Prange, *Miracle at Midway*. New York: McGraw-Hill, 1982. Noted history professor Gordon Prange has written excellent accounts of important events in the Pacific Theater. This depiction of the Battle of Midway is still one of the definitive texts.

Ward Rutherford, *Blitzkrieg 1940*. New York: Gallery Books, 1979. A well-illustrated history of the Nazi invasions of the Low Countries and France. Excellent for understanding how blitzkrieg tactics prevailed against a well-armed, well-defended nation like France.

Saburo Sakai, *Samurai!* New York: Ballantine Books, 1957. An engaging autobiography of one of Japan's most famous fighter aces; Sakai flew his Zero in many of the major battles of the Pacific conflict. A very useful book for those seeking to understand part of the Japanese perspective on the war.

Joseph A. Skiera, ed., *Aircraft Carriers in Peace and War*. New York: Franklin Watts, 1965. A collection of pieces describing the various uses of aircraft carriers. The sections on World War II are helpful.

Tanks and Weapons of World War II. New York: Beekman House, 1973. Part of the Beekman History of the World Wars Library, this volume offers an interesting collection of essays on various weapons of the war, including tanks, small arms, and rockets. Many drawings and photos accompany each essay.

Studs Terkel, *"The Good War": An Oral History of World War II*. New York: New Press, 1984. Terkel is noted for his compendiums of firsthand tales concerning historical events or periods during the twentieth century. The accounts are always vivid, as the examples in this volume of recollections of the Second World War prove.

Keith Wheeler, *Bombers over Japan*. Alexandria, VA: Time-Life Books, 1982. Another of the excellent Time-Life books from the WWII series. This volume covers the bombing raids over Japan. Filled with interesting information and pictures.

Earl Frederick Ziemke, *The Soviet Juggernaut*. Alexandria, VA: Time-Life Books, 1980. This Time-Life volume covers the turning of the tide in the Russian campaign, focusing on the Soviet advance through Poland, the Balkan nations, and Germany.

✫ Index ✫

★ Picture Credits ★

Cover Photo: Digital Stock

Archive Photos, 8, 69 (middle), 71, 83, 84

Archive Photos/Popperfoto, 96

Corbis, 11, 12 (right), 13, 19, 22, 39 (bottom), 45, 48, 56, 77, 78 (left), 93

Corbis/Owen Franken, 89

Corbis/Hulton-Deutsch Collection, 21, 31, 65, 80, 90, 91

Corbis/Museum of Flight, 46, 63

Corbis-Bettmann, 25, 34, 69 (bottom), 73 (left)

Digital Stock, 7, 9, 39 (top), 43, 44, 54 (both), 59, 61, 66, 85 (top), 92

FPG International, 10, 14, 17, 20, 26 (bottom), 27, 32, 35, 36, 40, 42 (both), 47, 60, 78 (right), 81

pixelpartners, 12 (left), 26 (top), 29, 50, 51, 52, 69 (top), 72, 73 (right), 74, 79, 85 (bottom)

Martha Schierholz, 64, 87